THE
ULTIMATE
FAMILY GIFT

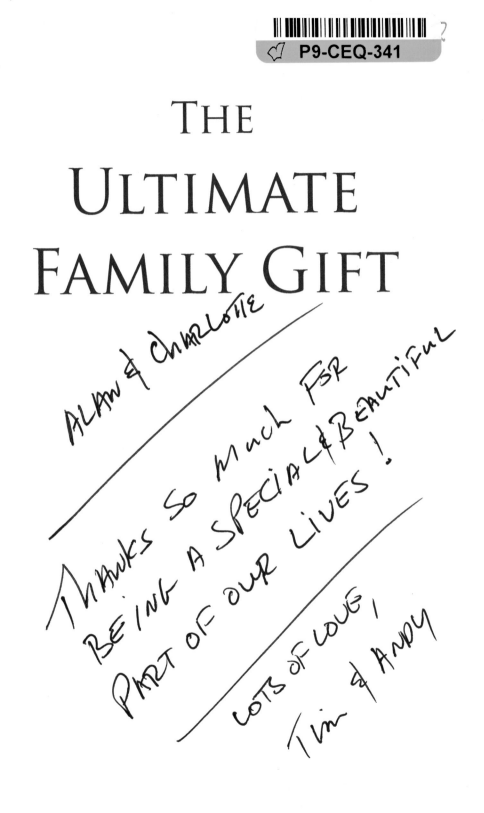

ALAN & CHARLOTTE

Thanks so much for being a special & beautiful part of our lives!

lots of love,

Tim & Andy

THE
ULTIMATE
FAMILY GIFT

Peace of Mind Through
Personalized
End-Of-Life Planning

TIM PELTON

Advantage®

Published by Advantage, Charleston, South Carolina.
Member of Advantage Media Group.

ADVANTAGE is a registered trademark and the Advantage colophon is a trademark of Advantage Media Group, Inc.

Printed in the United States of America.

ISBN: 978-159932-435-7
LCCN: 2013946475

This publication is designed to provide accurate and authoritative information in regard to the subject matter covered. It is sold with the understanding that the publisher is not engaged in rendering legal, accounting, or other professional services. If legal advice or other expert assistance is required, the services of a competent professional person should be sought.

Advantage Media Group is proud to be a part of the Tree Neutral® program. Tree Neutral offsets the number of trees consumed in the production and printing of this book by taking proactive steps such as planting trees in direct proportion to the number of trees used to print books. To learn more about Tree Neutral, please visit **www.treeneutral.com**. To learn more about Advantage's commitment to being a responsible steward of the environment, please visit **www.advantagefamily.com/green**

TreeNeutral

Advantage Media Group is a publisher of business, self-improvement, and professional development books and online learning. We help entrepreneurs, business leaders, and professionals share their Stories, Passion, and Knowledge to help others Learn & Grow. Do you have a manuscript or book idea that you would like us to consider for publishing? Please visit **advantagefamily.com** or call **1.866.775.1696**.

To my fallen fire service brothers Bob, JK, Pete E., and Pete G.

For giving me the motivation and passion to help others and to the inner sanctum of incredibly special people who have supported me on my life's journey.

TABLE OF CONTENTS

PREFACE

My goal with this book is to coach and motivate you to complete an important task, to take action on something you might find a challenge: planning the rest of your life, and more importantly what you would like to have happen after you pass away. This book is not about me, although you may think so as you start to read. *It is all about you.* It is simply my way to provide you with a call to action on critical matters that need your attention.

Life is a journey and it is full of opportunities. In the words of Ben Franklin, "Do not squander time for that is the stuff life is made of." Helping people has consistently been one of my primary objectives in life. I am going to take you on a personal journey that may be tempered by the fog of time but that is put into focus by looking through the prism of experience. We all have historical events that in hindsight we could have handled differently. Looking back, I have absolutely no regrets and "woulda, coulda, shoulda" simply isn't in my vocabulary. There is no return on investment in worrying about what could have been.

Life presents us with many unexpected opportunities. As this book goes to press, I am 65 years young, and I have had a wonderful, fascinating and rewarding life. Since age 60 is now the new 40, I still have a long way to go. As I relate to the experiences in my life in this book, last names have been respectfully eliminated to protect

the people involved and to not resurrect old memories that may be better left alone. Many incredibly special people have stood by me; they know who they are, and I am forever blessed to have known and worked with them. No regrets, but in hindsight I could've handled *a few things* a little differently.

In the 1950s, I grew up in western Massachusetts in a town called Pittsfield. It is a quintessential New England town where the four seasons of the year are unique, bucolic, and beautiful. It is a setting that would make Norman Rockwell proud.

While I truly didn't appreciate it at the time, I had the honor and privilege of meeting Norman Rockwell several times when I was growing up. My dad was a physician in Pittsfield and Norman Rockwell was one of his patients. In gratitude he did a portrait of my dad that is simply outstanding.

Norman often preferred to use local people as his models for a lot of his artwork, including the *Saturday Evening Post* covers. One time he asked me if I would like to be a model for him. I asked him what it entailed. He said I would need to stop by his studio in nearby Stockbridge and pose for him for some *Post* covers he was thinking about, and it would likely take a couple of days to get things worked out. I thought about it for a second and said, "Gee, I dunno. Thanks anyway," and I turned and left to go out and play a game of whiffle ball with the neighborhood kids. Talk about an opportunity lost.

While I will never know for sure, I have often been plagued by the thought that the March 15, 1958, *Saturday Evening Post* cover may be what Norman Rockwell had in mind. Maybe, just maybe, it could have been my backside on the *Post* cover instead of Eddie's.

Now the doctor in the picture is Doctor C, who was a friend and neighbor of Norman Rockwell. However, the doctor's office decor, the diplomas on the wall, and that bulky white scale look awfully familiar. It is disturbingly similar to my dad's office.

Fast forward to 1978. We were living in Bristol, Connecticut. There was a local sports commentator named Bill Rasmussen who was absolutely nuts about sports, sports broadcasting, and the University of Connecticut basketball program. If you follow college basketball at all, you know that UConn basketball is a huge enterprise in the state of Connecticut.

If you're old enough to recall the 1970s, you know that TV sets had only 12 channels. To state it more correctly, there was a knob with 12 channel positions on it, and you had to manually click between the 12 channels to get actual reception. There were only three networks: CBS, NBC, and ABC. Somewhere on that 12-channel dial you could get each of those three networks.

Back then, college sports on TV was nonexistent and Bill Rasmussen came up with the idea that maybe UConn basketball games could be broadcast throughout Connecticut using line-of-sight

TV antennas strategically placed throughout the state. A few years earlier in 1975, a division of RCA communications had launched the company's first communications satellite called Satcom1. Somewhere along the line, Bill Rasmussen came up with a business plan of not using line-of-sight television antennas in Connecticut but using satellite technology instead to broadcast television programming. Being a sports nut, he simply thought that everyone would want to watch sports, so why not watch it all day and all night?

At the same time, the ABC network was making a big push into sports to compete with the bulwark networks of NBC and CBS. We all remember the eloquence of ABC commentator Jim McKay, and who will ever forget Vinko Bogatja doing a horrific face plant fall off a ski jump in West Germany and suffering "the agony of defeat."

I had the opportunity to be interviewed by Bill Rasmussen following up on an advertisement he had placed. He was looking for a manager for a new business venture. He explained he wanted to take on and surpass NBC, CBS, and ABC, using satellite technology to broadcast sports around the country 24 hours a day. I concluded, in spite of his incredible enthusiasm, that tiny Bristol, Connecticut, was an unlikely location for such a venture. I respectfully responded that I was not interested. Bill Rasmussen did fulfill his vision and began broadcasting in September 1979. Today we know his venture as ESPN, and it is still based in Bristol, Connecticut. Another opportunity lost.

But who knew? We all make life defining decisions based upon the best information we have at the time, and we live with those decisions for better or for worse. I am pleased to say that I have had many more positive outcomes than those that were less than successful.

As you begin to leaf through this book, you will see that it is all about loving life. I'm going to take you on a very thought-provoking journey and ask you to think about the *rest* of your life and what you want to have happen when you pass away.

Now you may be thinking that this subject absolutely terrifies you and how can you even begin to talk about it? I get it; I understand. First of all, you should know you are not alone. Almost everyone I talk to finds it uncomfortable to discuss death and dying. I don't.

The sole purpose of this book is to make it easier for you to broach the subject of dying and to begin to discuss it with your family. Remember, this ultimate outcome is not about you. It is all about a plan for your family.

If you need a little help getting started, I have developed a short 20 page report called *The Nine Easy Ways To Start The Ultimate Conversation*. It is an easy read and available for free at my web site. Simply go to www.timpelton.com/9easyways to download a copy.

Why am I so passionate on the subject of *The Ultimate Family Gift?* As you will see reading through the book, I have seen dying and death at many levels. So many, in fact, I cannot possibly outline them all in this book. But my goal is to tell you something about my near misses, the passing of loved ones, and part of my challenging journey and experiences along the way.

Four times in my life I have gotten that dreaded phone call telling me that "time is short! If you want to say goodbye you better come now!" At each of those times it was often too late to talk.

Why I am the happiest guy in the world.

My reason for sharing each of these stories with you is to illustrate two important things: 1) end-of-life planning lifts a huge burden off your surviving family members, and 2) by the time you finish reading this book, you will have an enormous opportunity to provide your family with the consummate family gift, a roadmap to the ultimate outcome. The gift is the peace of mind of personalized end-of-life planning.

✓ HOT TIP ─────────────────

In my experience the closer people are to dying the more they appreciate what is most important in life.

─────────────────────────────

So sit back and enjoy a trip down memory lane and begin to understand better why I am so passionate about writing *The Ultimate Family Gift* and why I encourage you to become more engaged in caring for and planning for the rest of your own life. More importantly, planning for the ultimate outcome and peace of mind of those left behind may be the most important life decision that you will ever make.

Need a little help getting started? Take a look at my list of the 11 things you absolutely, positively must do BEFORE you die. It is also available for free on my website at www.timpelton.com/11things. Download your copy now.

ACKNOWLEDGMENTS

"I've said it before, but it is absolutely true: my mother gave me my drive, but my father gave me my dreams."

—Liza Minnelli

Now, truth be told, with all the hundreds of books I have read, I never really paid much attention to the Acknowledgments section. I simply didn't get it. After working on this book, I do.

The Acknowledgments section allows me to reflect and thank all the people in my life who had a direct impact on the successful completion of this book. They gave me the compassion, the understanding, and the motivation to complete this effort.

I want to thank my family: Dad, Mom, my older brother, Peter, and my older sister, Deb. Unfortunately, they have all passed away due to health-related maladies. I am the sole survivor of a family of five. I was blessed with a take-away from each funeral that, in turn, motivated me to not only start but also complete this project.

Vacationing on the New Jersey Shore

I am forever grateful to my business partner, Bob, who is the visionary of our partnership. He encouraged me and coached me to create this book when I wasn't quite sure I had it in me. It's amazing how special relationships grow. Bob and I first met

back on April 23, 1987, as charter members of a special team to help emergency service personnel manage extremely stressful incidents. We first met when an apartment building under construction in Bridge-port, CT, collapsed, resulting in the deaths of 28 construction workers. Who could predict years later that we would become close friends and business partners.

Words cannot express my indebtedness to my wonderful bride Andrea, affectionately known as Andy. We first met at the airport in Kansas City on August 26, 1966. You do the math. We have known each other for a long time. Through all those years she has believed in me and supported everything I wanted to do. She is my loving spouse, my conscience, my reality check, and my best friend. Andy is the genesis for this book. The day I pass away, she will pull out our copy of the comprehensive end-of-life plan we built together and she will implement it.

And lastly, to my beautiful daughter, Jennifer. February 25, 1983, will always be the happiest day of my life. That's the day I brought Jen into this world, literally, in the delivery room at New Britain General Hospital. Every day since has been filled with joy, happiness, and accomplishments with Jen. She has been a key editor of this book. She is out of college and all grown up now, but she will always be Daddy's little girl.

This book is about loving life and what should happen when you pass away.

Let's begin with my story and my family, but I want you to think about your family.

 HOT TIP

Throughout the book you will see this symbol to highlight a particular topic worth noting. The hot tip here is that as we start out on our journey together to discuss things for you to think about during the rest of your life, I have tied together part of my story with a planning strategy that I'd like you consider. Read on and enjoy.

Let's begin by going back to the early years.

CHAPTER ONE

The Beginning

"Accept everything about yourself—I mean everything. You are you and that is the beginning and the end—no apologies, no regrets."

—HENRY A. KISSINGER

As we get started I want to tell you why I am so passionate about this book and share with you many of the unique aspects of my life that motivated me to write *The Ultimate Family Gift.*

My childhood was pretty normal. At least I think it was normal. Isn't it perfectly normal for a seven-year-old boy to climb out a sec-

ond-story window, jump to a tree, shimmy down, and go outside and play with his friends? I think so. You might say I'm a bit of a risk taker—in the words of Robert Frost, "Two roads diverged in a wood, and I took the one less traveled by, and that has made all the difference."

I was the youngest of three children. I want to take a moment to tell you a little more about my family and some of the events in my life that motivated me to write *The Ultimate Family Gift*.

My brother Peter was the oldest, and in the middle was my sister, Deb. Pete was a really interesting guy. His basic principle was to ponder why a perfectly good education should get in the way of having fun. I am reminded of the scene from the classic movie *Animal House* when references are made to the "German" bombing of Pearl Harbor. When you look up the term *truant child* in Webster's dictionary, the text will read, "See Pelton, Peter." The thing I admire about Pete the most is that he lived his life *his* way, and how he relished it.

Deb, on the other hand, was the perfect daughter—I think I've got all this right and if not, I'm pretty close—school valedictorian, lead in the school play, editor of the school newsletter, excellent grades—you get the point. She was the shining star of the troika of Pelton kids.

And then there was me. This is where I learned a valuable lesson.

LIFE LESSON NUMBER ONE:
FLY BELOW THE RADAR SCREEN.

Do not be an academic standout with either perfect grades or failing grades. Do not be high maintenance or a trouble maker. Fly right in the middle and you can get away with murder. Plus, I had the advantage of two siblings going before me to "break in" my parents with all the crazy stuff children do.

Now that doesn't mean you can't be stupid, because I certainly did my fair share of *really* stupid things. However, my primary objective was never to get caught. My dad and I had an informal but mutually accepted understanding. Dad said he would give me a little more latitude versus my brother and sister. But—and there is always a but—if you ever screw up and get caught, it will be a very, very bad day. So I was pretty successful at not getting caught and not being stupid—but not every time.

The year was 1956. It was a beautiful clear autumn day in New England. The air was cool and crisp with the wonderful smell of burning leaves. It was Election Day. Kids were out of school and Eisenhower was running for president.

I begged my mother to let me go watch her vote and she said okay, as long as I was ready to go by eleven o'clock sharp. So I jumped into my Keds Red Ball sneakers, threw on a pair of blue jeans, buttoned up a heavy, itchy, Woolrich, plaid shirt, and like all good eight-year-olds, I went outside to play. One of the neighbors had raked leaves into a huge pile right next to a fence. So what greater joy could there be for an eight-year-old than to jump off a fence repeatedly into a large leaf pile. Unfortunately, I did not know that there was a big rock beneath the leaf pile and when doing a cannonball leap into the leaf pile, I broke my leg. Then it started. I could hear my mother frantically beeping the horn of our 1952 Plymouth Concord and shouting, "It's time to go!"

The fear of the wrath of not being on time at eleven o'clock sharp far outweighed the excruciating pain I was feeling in my leg. She eventually drove down the driveway and saw me in the next-door neighbor's yard. With tears running down my face, I was in pure agony, and she thought I was faking it for being late. Her compassionate response was, "Yeah yeah sure. Get in the car!"

Now the car happened to be an old Plymouth that we called "The Rock" because it was built like one. You may recall in the older cars there was a hump in the middle of the floor in the back seat where the driveshaft beneath the car connected the transmission to the rear wheels. I dragged myself unassisted onto the floor of the backseat where I put my leg up on the hump. I saw that while my leg below the knee was resting on the hump, my leg was making a strange angle and my ankle was on the floor. My initial thought was that this was definitely not good.

I pleaded that I was in too much agony to go watch my mother vote. She was unconcerned and told me to stay in the car (you could leave kids in cars in the old days), and she said we would go get my leg checked out when she was done voting. Well, we went to the hospital and X-rays were taken, and she was truly stunned by the reality of what I had done, and that I actually did have a broken leg. Needless to say, I was able to milk that sympathy for years.

This is not to say that I didn't have loving parents. They were outstanding, and we had a close-knit family, but things were different back then. My dad was a physician. He kept unique hours. He was up and out at 5 a.m. to make rounds at the hospital, saw his patients for the duration of the day, came home, had dinner, and then went off to bed.

To some extent I competed with his patients for his time. But I understood it and accepted it, and it helped shape me into the person that I am today, knowing that *we were both put on this planet to help people.* In my lengthy career in health care and the fire service, I have been able to help people that I know and people that I have never met before. One of my core values is to be able to look in the mirror every day and answer the question: Whom did you help today?

Thanks, Dad.

My public safety aspirations came relatively early in life, and I knew that being a firefighter would be part of it. I went to elementary school at the Redfield School—and yes I walked to school, two miles uphill both ways (just kidding). Actually, I did walk to school every day and it was about a mile each way.

One year there was a field trip to the Pittsfield Fire Department. The firehouse itself was a huge brick building with massive doors. It was just a little bit bigger than the Empire State building in New York City. The red fire trucks were about the size of two school buses and when the firemen, who happened to be the biggest men on the planet, came to greet us, they slid down a brass fire pole that was at least 200 feet long. It was the neatest thing I had ever seen. The frosting on the cake came when an alarm came in from dispatch. The men said, "Kids, stand over here and don't move." The men all jumped into tall rubber boots, put on huge black coats, and donned enormous leather fire helmets. The doors flew open as we put our hands over our ears, sirens started to scream, and the trucks left with

a roar. On that day, at the age of eight, I was hooked, and I knew that several years later I would fulfill my dream of becoming a fireman.

But one's career in public safety can start early. And there was nothing more prestigious for a fifth-grader at the Redfield School than to be a crosswalk guard. You got to wear a huge white sash across your chest and a bright silver badge and carry a red flag on a stick that was used to control traffic and pedestrians. While I had no idea what hormones were, I did know that girls really liked the crosswalk guards, and like anything else, you needed to compete for the position of crosswalk guard by writing a short essay. Well, I didn't make it. You see, back in school in the dark ages, we were taught to spell "fon-et-ick-al-ly." I was crushed and, adding insult to injury, the job went to my ex-best friend, Mike. Well, he stayed my best friend, but we didn't talk for a couple days while I got over the disappointment.

LIFE LESSON NUMBER TWO:
THINGS DON'T ALWAYS TURN OUT THE WAY YOU WANT THEM TO.

I first learned about the pain of death at the age of nine. It wasn't a family member or relative, but, to a nine-year-old boy, it was something much more important: my dog, Prince. Prince was an Airedale, black and tan, and scruffy, with a bobbed tail. He and I

really didn't have time to go to dog obedience school, and it showed. But he was the love of my life, and he was struck and killed by a car. To a nine-year-old child it is unconscionable that a car driver could be so irresponsible and so callous as to hit a dog. Note that irresponsibility on the part of the dog does not enter into this discussion.

I was sad for a long time. Until then, life had been pretty straight forward. If you brushed your teeth every day and said the Pledge of Allegiance at school, life would always be good.

Well, not entirely good. Let's go back to being young and foolish. No. Let's call it being young and stupid.

Remember I talked about the importance of not getting caught? Well, as Tom Hanks said in the movie *Forrest Gump,* "Stupid is what stupid does." As you will see, sometimes being stupid got in the way of my priority of not getting caught.

It's now wintertime and there is a fresh batch of new-fallen snow on the ground, and it is snow that has the perfect consistency for making snowmen…and snowballs. I realize that it probably wasn't a good idea to throw snowballs at moving cars from your front yard. As I look back on this incident I really ponder how I could have been that stupid.

Life lesson number one: *Fly below the radar screen* somehow got lost that day.

Long story short: one particular snowball that I launched with a precision similar to firing a heat-seeking missile from a drone in Afghanistan slammed into a driver's side window. There was a screech of tires. The window rolled down, and someone shouted "Timmy Pelton stop this now! Don't make me call your father." Cold sweat ran down my spine. Who was that person and, more importantly, how did she know it was me? (Duh!)

In the '50s there was no fate short of death that was worse than when someone called your father. Even today I shudder at the words. It was not the fear of potential corporal punishment but the saddened eyes of disappointment that was truly painful. Fortunately the call was never made—whew!

So since no complaint was made and that particular snowball throwing model was not particularly successful, I did what all resourceful young boys did: I went to snowball-throwing Plan B .4 .6. In other words, I changed my location. It just so happened there was a small park opposite the St. Theresa Church in Pittsfield that was located high above South Street. Notice the word *above*. We could launch snowballs from an elevated position, and as all military strategists know, having an elevated position is the best. We could lob a snowball on a high arc, time it perfectly, and have it hit a passing car with the clear benefit that we were out of sight.

One particular evening we were honing our skills, and the only way to practice our timing was to work with the oncoming headlights of the car. I had my timing down pat and let one fly. Again the trajectory was perfect. It was only the outcome that was imperfect.

The snowball hit the car in the middle of the roof, right next to the light on top of the police car. Pure terror struck my heart. I looked for brake lights to come on and a screech of tires and I was ready to make my exit, but nothing happened. The police car simply proceeded down the road as if nothing had happened. "Hmmm, pretty cool," I thought. As we basked in the glory of hitting a police car, we thought nothing more about it. A short time later, our strategic position was suddenly illuminated by a police car spotlight of at least 57,000,000 candlepower! I was blinded! All I could hear was a deep voice bellowing "Don't move!" As I have mentioned before, flying below the radar screen is one of my important life lessons. Getting caught by the cops for throwing snowballs would not play out well on the home front.

It was time to move. Olympic high hurdler Bob Hayes had nothing on me that night and I took off like a shot. I seem to recall there was a six-foot-high fence around the park, and I think I hurled myself over the fence without even climbing it. I was absolutely terrified. And I know now, as an adult, that the cop probably drove away chuckling to himself. What he didn't know was that I had the runs for two days.

Growing up in the '50s really was a good time. No, we didn't have Nintendo, we didn't have X-Box, we didn't have computers, and we didn't have cell phones. There were not 150 channels on cable, no video movies or DVDs, no surround sound, no CDs, and no Internet. But if you played it just right on your black-and-white TV, you might get up to three channels if you had the tinfoil placed just right on the rabbit-ear TV antennas. And if not, we had friends outside and went to find them.

We made up games with broom sticks and tennis balls or whiffle balls (remember those?). And although we were told it would happen, we never poked out any eyes. We would try and build go carts out of bicycle parts, boxes, wheelbarrow parts, and whatever we could find and ride down the hill. Unfortunately, with our fledgling engineering skills, we discovered we had forgotten about brakes, and after running into the bushes a couple times and maybe a parked car or two, we learned how to solve our mechanical problems. What a concept.

Life was good in spite of the fact that Mom always said that the mercurochrome would only sting "a little bit" as it was dabbed on a scrape or wound. Yeah, right! The sting of white heat is still easy to recall. (Hmmm, maybe with all the current flap over the CIA water-boarding terrorists to gain information, perhaps they should consider just going back to using a little mercurochrome.)

Anyway, we were outside all day. Why? Because we simply weren't allowed in the house. We rode our bikes everywhere. Being outside all day where no one was able to reach us was just fine. I loved cruising on my blue Columbia bike with its big white-wall tires. We rode bikes all day and didn't wear helmets, and the only rule was to be home by five o'clock for dinner. There was a huge General Electric plant in Pittsfield when I was growing up, and we could hear its five-o'clock whistle all over town. Again, it was a fate worse than death if you heard the low moan of the whistle and you were not home.

Did we have 10-speed, synchronized-gear-ratio bikes? No. Did our bikes require special shoes for locking in the pedals? No. Probably a good thing that there were no gears. If you had to go up a hill, you simply stood up and peddled harder. Now, if your feet came off the pedals as you peddled uphill, and you crashed down on the cross bar of the frame, that was a whole new type of pain.

Talk about the need to be cool! There was nothing better than taking a couple of baseball cards and a clothes pin off the clothesline to rev up your bike and pretend you were Marlon Brando in *The Wild One.* Of course, the real tragedy was how many Roger Maris or Mickey Mantle baseball cards I chewed up in the process of trying to be cool. By the way, those baseball cards can go for up to $3,000 each today. That sure would buy a lot of Jujubes.

In those days we rode around in cars that didn't have seatbelts. Remember I mentioned the Plymouth Rock? To this day I am convinced that Plymouth made Sherman tanks during World War II and went back to making cars after the war simply by replacing the tank treads with four tires. The dashboards were hard and had all kinds of projectiles sticking out ready to scrape your face off. There were knobs for tuning the radio, adjusting the fan, adjusting the heater, and opening the glove compartment. The only safety item was Mom's safety arm for quick stops. In the event of a quick stop, Mom's arm would shoot out across your chest and try to hold you in place. And of course if you got hurt when your head ricocheted off the dashboard, it was your fault for "calling shotgun" in the first place.

Now for the ill-informed, the position of shotgun is the passenger seat in the front a car. This came from watching all the Westerns on TV including *Hopalong Cassidy, Gunsmoke, The Lone Ranger,* and many others, in which security on a stagecoach was a man who carried a shotgun and sat next to the driver. Ah, those were the days—"Hi Ho, Silver…away!"

Again, being a bit of a risk taker, I loved being pulled behind a car on a sled in the wintertime. Somehow the subject of CO (carbon monoxide) poisoning never came up. Other than being run over by another car, having your car reverse direction and back over you, sliding under the rear bumper should the car brake suddenly, or having the centrifugal force phenomenon with its crack-the-whip effect throw you into a tree, it really wasn't that hazardous. And it remains one of my fondest memories of growing up in the Berkshires in the wintertime.

Of course, it was not so cool if you could be suckered into sticking your tongue on the metal frame of your American Flyer sled on a cold winter's day. Now, I can say that I was never suckered into that position, but I cannot say that I did not make that proposal to others. I can still see the pools of drool accumulating as I encouraged my colleagues to run looking for warm water to get our friend unstuck. I had also heard of variations of this theme such as sticking your tongue on a metal flagpole in the wintertime, but I must confess I never saw that happen.

Back to being stupid.

Now what is your immediate reaction to a sign that reads, "Wet paint" or "Wet cement"? Obviously, you're tempted to validate the sign, much to the displeasure of the painter or the guy pouring the sidewalk. So when, during winter, a mother warns against playing by the river because it's dangerous, what does any high-spirited young boy do? Of course. He goes down by the river to play.

A few words about the Housatonic River in Pittsfield are in order. The river ran all the way through town and we lived near it. I grew up next to the river, caught frogs, threw mud at my friends, and did everything a normal boy would do growing up by a river. As mentioned before, General Electric had a huge complex in Pittsfield where, among other things, they built transformers. And there was a long history of allegations that GE deposited waste oil containing PCBs (polychlorinated biphenyls) into the Housatonic River and contaminated it. When the environmental movement caught on in the '80s and '90s, there was a big movement to have GE clean up the river because of the alleged contamination with PCBs and the negative impact that had on the environment, including fish in the river, and people living near the river.

Despite the fact that studies have alleged PCB contamination might have a negative health impact, I did every kind of activity you would expect a young boy to do along Housatonic River in the '50s, and because I have experienced no noticeable effects from the prolonged exposure to the PCB contamination, I question whether the reaction to PCBs might be overrated.

So back to why "Don't go play by the river" is important. I was bundled up against a cold winter's day and the snow crunched softly under my feet. As most young lads like to do, I decided to experiment. Just how far out on the ice could I go before the ice would start to crack? I vividly remember to this day what happened next.

I fell through the ice, but I was able to grab the edge of the ice while the river flow was trying to draw me beneath it. The edge of the ice held and I was able to slowly pull myself up and haul myself out. I sat there on the river bank shivering. I wasn't shivering because of a near-death experience because I didn't even know what that meant. I wasn't shivering because I was cold and wet. I was shivering because I knew that I was in deep trouble. I did exactly the opposite of what I was strictly told not to do and I was going to get caught. How could I possibly get home and sneak into the house without Mom finding out? It was a very perplexing problem.

What's interesting is that more than 50 years later I still remember every detail of what transpired. I was in a blue snowsuit. I had red boots on. I had wool mittens with a white moose woven into the mittens and a knit cap that was tied under my chin by yarn straps with balls on the end of each strap. I was soaked from my chest down and the moisture was starting to crystallize on the snowsuit.

In other words, I needed to make up a story that fit the situation. I told my mother that I was playing in a large puddle, and yes, I was stupid, and yes, I was all wet, and yes, I felt very bad about it. I was severely chastised and told "You really need to be more careful, Tim. You could catch your death of a cold." It was only years later that I realized how poignant that remark was. I think she bought the story because we never spoke of it again. But as I got older and thought about the story, it is incredibly fortunate that it didn't turn into a tragedy and they found my body sometime in the spring.

This is one more reason for me to realize that I was put on the planet to help people. I was stupid and yet lived to tell about it. This theme was to become an inspiration.

Let's go back to Redfield Elementary School. In the 1950s the Soviet Union was considered the Evil Empire, long before Ronald Reagan coined the phrase. The world powers were building up a huge stockpile of nuclear weapons and the school system thought it would be appropriate to conduct civil defense duck-and-cover drills at school. Even at this young age I began to grasp the concept that, from time to time, the federal government may not always know exactly what the hell it is talking about.

You see, somehow, I could never quite grasp the logic of the duck-and-cover drills. The federal logic was that if there were a nuclear attack, glass windows would shatter and the glass would blow into the classroom, endangering all the kids in it. So we needed to practice crawling under our desks and putting our arms over our head—duck and cover. The fact that the whole building was going to be vaporized somehow escaped the adult mind. I just didn't get it.

But I did have an evening when I truly thought nuclear armageddon had occurred. The Pittsfield General Electric complex developed the Poseidon missile for nuclear submarines. So we were all convinced that GE, as part of the U. S. military-industrial complex, was a potential target of a Soviet nuclear attack. At Christmas in 1958, as so many houses did, we put electric candles on all the window sills to be festive. Rather than unplug them every night, we simply gave the bulb a couple twists until they turned off. Our house was less than energy efficient. If the wind blew in from a certain direction, you could watch the curtains move. One night, in came a winter storm, and it was enough to jiggle the light bulb in the electric candle, and the light came on. In those days the bulbs were orange to simulate the color of an orange candle flame. Well, in the middle the night, my room lit up in a brilliant orange flash, and I truly thought that the Soviets had taken out GE with a nuclear attack, and I had somewhere between three and four seconds before the shockwave would hit me. Obviously, the shockwave didn't hit, we were not destroyed, and life moved on. But I share this story to underscore the paranoia of how growing up under the threat of a nuclear holocaust shaped my sense of reality.

I "survived again" and was encouraged to continue with my mission to help people.

Now I'm not suggesting that while in elementary school I was an instigator of trouble because, as I say:

LIFE RULE NUMBER ONE (REVISITED):
FLY BELOW THE RADAR SCREEN.

But out on the school playground everything is fair game. Whether it was an overzealous game of dodge ball, claiming squatters' rights on the monkey bars, or arguing that my bike is better than your bike, boys will be boys.

As I said, there was no fate worse than when someone said, "Do I need to call your father?" The next worst fate, worse than death itself, was when my fourth-grade teacher would rap her ring on the open window while looking at the playground and shout, "Timmy Pelton come here right now!" Oh man! I was dead meat. While I clearly believed I was innocent of all charges, this was not going to be a trial by jury. Inevitably I would be assigned to clapping erasers after school.

Long before there were whiteboards with felt tip markers or digitized smart boards, there were blackboards with chalk and erasers. One of the most demeaning and socially unacceptable situations was to be kept after school, and to be kept after school to clap erasers… well, that was the worst. And God forbid you should ever try and be cute and clap the erasers on the side of a red brick school building. My teacher promised that if I ever tried to do that, I would be thrown into the bowels of the coal-fired boiler in the school basement and be instantly incinerated, and I didn't doubt the legitimacy of that threat.

By now, I hope you can see that my childhood was pretty normal, or least I think it was normal. We all did stupid stuff and hopefully most of us dodged a bullet and suffered no major repercussions most of the time. It could be said that I did okay in school. But in hindsight it's really hard for me to judge because report cards only showed an S for satisfactory and a U for unsatisfactory. If there were a lot more Ss than Us, all was right with the world.

Now be nice to your sister!

LIFE LESSON NUMBER THREE:
ACADEMIC SMARTS DON'T ALWAYS HELP, BUT STREET SMARTS WILL ALWAYS GET YOU BY.

CHAPTER TWO

The Teenage Years

"I get letters from kids, teenagers, and young girls who just want to be Mac. I've had quite a few people actually say that they're going to become a marine or a JAG lawyer because of me … the character. I think that's pretty cool!"

—CATHERINE BELL, ACTRESS, JAG TV SERIES

Now, as a teenager, my public safety mission and persona really began to take shape. I had always liked being around water (even when I fell in the river), and I spent part of the '60s being a lifeguard both in Massachusetts and in New Jersey.

Ah yes, the summer of '66. Now, that was a great summer. I was a lifeguard on the beautiful beaches on the New Jersey shore in a small town called Bay Head. I was fit and trim, having come off a season of high-school lacrosse, and I was working and sucking up the sun on the Jersey shore. Life was good. I had a Honda 250 cc trail bike motorcycle, I had discovered beer, and I had a girlfriend. Brad Pitt couldn't hold a candle to the job that I had. Did I mention that being a lifeguard on the Jersey shore is a perfect chick magnet job? And when a good-looking brunette asks you, "So what time is low tide?" for the fourth time, she is either not too bright (always a distinct possibility), or she is making a play for you. Either way there were some very interesting conversations.

We kept an informal tally of our lifeguarding duties. A "rescue" meant you made a significant difference in someone's life, a "pluck" was helping a child or someone knocked down by a wave near shore, and a "recon" was an attractive young lady in fabricated distress. During my tenure on the Jersey shore I had 11 rescues (2 very serious) and all successful, fortunately; 29 plucks; and countless recons.

The job did have some redeeming value.

But by the summer of 1966 I knew that I was destined to help people who otherwise might not be able to help themselves.

Next, came college. I attended school at Park University in Kansas City, and I learned an interesting lesson in perspective. I was the typical cocky kid from the East Coast who thought that everyone in KC probably drove a pickup truck with a gun rack, and that they rolled up the sidewalks at 7 p.m. What I discovered were people who were incredibly sincere and down to earth, drove Ford mustangs or Chevy Corvairs (if you dared), and KC was the cultural center of the middle of the country.

When I first started receiving mail from the school as part of the enrollment process, their letterhead tagline was, "The best four years of your life." I thought it was a catchy phrase but one that I really didn't put much credence in. But looking back, I was one happy camper (and I also met my future wife on my first day at Park on August 26, 1966).

However, I almost blew it. Here we go, back to being stupid again. When the first-semester grades came out, my parents made it perfectly clear that if the current direction of my academic pursuits were to continue, there would be a serious modification of my college plan. Message received. I got back on the horse, performed well, and I remain proud of my tenure at Park.

I majored in physics and math. My goal was to graduate and go to work for NASA, and little did I know when we landed a man on the moon in 1969 that the scope of the NASA program would be severely modified and cut back. Therefore my original plan was simply not going to work out, and as it turned out, Uncle Sam had another plan for me anyway.

Academically, I'm proud to say that I was awarded the Outstanding Physics Award for stellar performance for a graduating senior majoring in physics. At graduation I proudly acknowledged and accepted my academic achievement. Now, I told you that street smarts in my mind are always better than academic smarts. So then it's only fair to share with you that I was the <u>only</u> graduating senior majoring in physics that year. They had to give somebody the award and I was the lucky candidate.

LIFE LESSON NUMBER THREE (REVISITED): *ACADEMIC SMARTS DON'T ALWAYS HELP, BUT STREET SMARTS WILL ALWAYS GET YOU BY.*

Allow me to share with you another application of street smarts that involves several nostalgic items, none of which still exist today. In packages my parents would occasionally send from home, there would always be a roll of quarters to call home and check in from the pay phone. But why waste perfectly good quarters on a call home when that same currency could buy beer? A six-pack of Schlitz, the beer that made Milwaukee famous, went for 99 cents. However there was still the obligation to occasionally touch base with the home front.

In the late '60s, college dorms all had one payphone per hallway. There were no individual phones in dorm rooms. There weren't any cell phones. There was just one pay phone at the end of the hall for everybody to use. Now being an ever-resourceful college student, I discovered that you could fool the payphone by inserting a narrow strip of plastic down the quarter slot when the operator came on to say, "Twenty-five cents more for the next three minutes." Remember those days? Now, where can you find a narrow strip of plastic to slip down the quarter slot in the payphone? Back in the 1960s, in every seat pocket on an airline, was a thin piece of plastic about 3" x 6" that was marked "Occupied." It was to be left on your seat when you went to the restroom or walked around the plane. At the time, Trans World Airlines (TWA) was a major player in the airline business. The thickness of a TWA "Occupied" seat sign was perfect for cutting into a strip about three-quarters of an inch wide, and sliding into the quarter slot every time the operator said, "Twenty-five cents more, please." I am not sure why, but the operator never listened for the clink of a descending quarter. Instead, she looked for the electronic signal that signaled something had dropped down the quarter slot. Anyway, from my perspective it was a great system because (1) it kept me in beer, and (2) Ma Bell could afford the loss.

Going to college in the '60s was a great time. I had learned my lesson to keep off my parents' radar by being strong enough to perform academically yet not be so consumed with my academic pursuits as to throw off my all-important social demands. Life was good. And in the words of rock legend Stephen Stills, "If you can't be with the one you love, honey, love the one you're with." Life truly was good.

The campus at Park went through an interesting metamorphosis from 1966 to 1970. In my freshman year, alcohol was strictly forbidden on campus. Girls' dorms were very reminiscent of the scene from *Animal House* when Otter and the guys went on their field trip to Emily Dickenson College. You would meet your date in the lobby and the front door to the dorm was hermetically sealed like a bank vault at midnight. Fortunately, all these barriers simply required more creative thinking. It was a question of the need to modify, adapt, and overcome school policies.

To overcome these barriers, our solution was a "woodsie." Think of it as a beach blanket party in a Missouri farmer's field. A blanket, a case of beer, your girlfriend/date (but not both), and a roaring campfire meant a good time was to be had by all. It was not unusual to consolidate resources and have 10–12 couples join in for a night of fun and frolic, watching the "submarine races" on the Missouri river. I was truly perplexed when some of the ladies who joined us complained that no submarines came by, let alone had a race. (Yikes!) "Have another beer, honey!"

Benjamin Franklin said, "You may delay, but time will not." Several things happen at midnight. Cinderella's coach turns into a pumpkin and the bank vault door on the girls' dorm closes. It was not unusual for me to then scale the side of a two-story, brick, girl's dormitory, rap on the window, and wake my date's roommate so she would go downstairs and open the front door.

It is unfortunate that Park did not have an engineering degree as part of its curriculum. Had it offered one, my colleagues would not have looked to me, the physics major, to make a plumbing repair in our dorm. As most of us know, campus maintenance personnel are often slow to make repairs. Men's college dorm bathrooms back then were really just locker rooms with back-to-back, 50-year-old, marble sinks, multiple showers housing various microbiological experiments, and a row of toilet stalls. In the middle of it all was a floor drain to capture excess water that had spilled from the sinks, dysfunctional shower curtains, and the overflow from the occasional log jams that occurred in a toilet.

Over the course of time and human events the floor drain became clogged, and there was always an inch or so of standing water about five to six-feet wide over the floor drain. Repeated requests to the campus maintenance folks to make the needed repairs were not successful, and, as always happens, when we got back to the dorm, there was an event that broke the camel's back. One of the guys had had a tough night at a party and needed to "drive the porcelain bus." Unfortunately, during his episode he missed the toilet and the floor was covered with a combination of Boone's Farm apple wine and what we suspected was the residue of several sticks of Slim Jim's beef jerky. With the floor drain blocked, there was no way to wash away the mess. As the resident pseudo-engineer-want-to-be, I was immediately approached for a consultation to remedy this travesty of plumbing injustice. I had also returned from the same party, and the solution in my head was immediately clear. The blockage in the floor drain was highly likely the culprit and the clog had to be removed.

An exhaustive search for a plumber's snake to free the clog was unsuccessful. However, a cherry bomb was discovered. A cherry bomb is a big firecracker on steroids. Being somewhat familiar with this pyrotechnic device, I thought it might do the trick. As a physics major, I was well versed in the equation: force equals mass times acceleration ($F = M \times A$). However, I was concerned that the specific gravity of water at room temperature was around 0.998, which meant that the cherry bomb might float and not get close enough to the clog. Again, the answer was intuitively obvious. By wrapping a few nails around the cherry bomb, the specific gravity issue would successfully be resolved.

With great fanfare, the rusty cover of the floor drain was removed, and the cherry bomb was ignited and dropped precisely into the middle of the drain. Small bubbles arose through the stagnant water in the drain. Nothing happened. Twelve close friends anxiously looked on. Then, 4.8935 seconds later, there was a muffled noise, followed by a sound similar to a World War II depth charge going off. A huge geyser of water, hair, and brown/green slime found only in floor drains went everywhere. It hit the ceiling above the drain, covered all four walls, and spattered on all the participants watching this historic event. Soon after, we were thrilled to hear the sucking sound of the men's room "pond" draining through the now-cleared floor drain. Cheers and accolades arose from the nearby crowd. Only when the moment of glory had passed and things began to return to normal did we hear the screams from the bathroom of the ladies dorm one floor below. Upon closer observation, it could be seen that the clog had indeed been removed along with bottom of the cast iron floor drain and a portion of the ladies bathroom ceiling below. Never has anyone's fall from grace been so rapid. In turning around and looking for support from my learned colleagues, no one was in sight! All that could be heard were feet running down the hall, accompanied by hysterical laughter. In conclusion, there were consequences of course, and I had to do campus maintenance work to pay for the total cost of repairs. But my legacy of do-it-yourself plumbing repairs and my intuitive engineering skills remains intact and is savored every time I get together with my close college friends.

Looking back, they truly might've been the best four years of my life: three meals a day, a roof over my head, women, beer, parents 1,500 miles away, the love of my life and future wife, and a cherry bomb legacy.

At the conclusion of my college experiences, the school changed in so many ways. By 1970, dorms were open all the time, more students were allowed to have cars on campus, and drugs began to encroach as the mind-liberating, free-spirit release, replacing alcohol. It was the '70s man, like, awesome dude. Truth be told, I think it was more rewarding in the mid-60s when the challenges of dating, drinking, dorm access, and having transportation needed to be overcome through creative planning and the assistance of great friends.

But all good things must come to an end.

Chapter Three

The Navy Years

"I wouldn't trade those 10 years for anything.
The navy taught me a lot of things. It molded me as a
man, and I made a lot of wonderful friends."

—Ernest Borgnine

In 1970 I won the lottery. It is the only lottery I have ever won. It was the draft lottery based on one's birthday to determine who would be called to active duty in the military. My number was 35. Good old Uncle Sam made that commitment for me. I started to discuss the situation with my dad and we briefly discussed options. I knew he'd served on Guadalcanal in World War II, and while I could never get him to discuss it, he was proud to have served. He instilled in me the pride and esprit de corps that comes with serving in the military.

We decided that my love of being on the water and my need to serve my country would be best served by my going into the navy. My plan was simple. I would graduate from Park, work through

Dad

the summer, and attend naval officer candidate school in the fall. Just before graduation, I received my induction notice into military service and went through the orientation and physical exam process at the military induction center located in Kansas City.

Now, at this point in my life, I was still pretty cocky. I'd survived my youth, survived the teenage years, survived college, and had a bucket full of street smarts. How then could I have been so stupid? Here we go again.

It was late in the summer when I got my notice to report for military service. I went to a local navy recruiter and explained that my officer candidate school (OCS) application was still in process and I was supposed to report to the navy later that year. He said "No problem, Son. We'll get you started as an enlisted recruit, and they'll just come get you when they're ready for you at OCS." I thought, "*That* makes sense to me," and Lord knows how I could have been so stupid. I am also confident that this navy recruiter, upon his retirement, either became a sleaze-ball, used-car salesman or a crooked politician, which is pretty much the same thing.

I reported to the U.S. Navy training center in Great Lakes, Illinois, in January 1971, which turned out to be the coldest January on record in the twentieth century. You really don't know what cold is until you're standing in formation at 0530 hours, in dungarees, in Illinois, in January, with stiff winter winds whipping off Lake Michigan. Over time it became crystal clear that no one was ever going to come get me and reassign me to officer candidate school.

Okay, if I was to become a naval officer, I would need to start over again, and this time I had learned my lesson (or so I thought). I submitted an application to attend OCS, and I knew that there would be physicals, oral boards, and interviews. My eyesight has always been poor. I have needed glasses for as long as I can remember.

I knew that the vision test for the OCS application was going to be a problem. So one day, I made my way to sick bay, complaining of back pain, and while there, I was able to write down and memorize part of the eye chart on the wall. I memorized the chart down to the line for 20/30 vision. I then went through several oral interviews of why I wanted to become a naval officer. A typical question would be:

If you are the gunnery officer on a destroyer and your orders were to open fire on a hamlet on the shores of Viet Nam, how would you feel about that?

Answer:

Sir, if there is a strategic advantage determined by my superior officers that a military strike is required to either protect military personnel or advance our efforts in Viet Nam, so be it. Lock, load, and fire for effect!

Everything was going great until I got to the old man, the commanding officer of the Great Lakes Naval Training Center, Captain Bligh. His gold braid went all the way up the arm on his uniform, and he had salt under his eyebrows after serving 84 years on the USS *Neverdock*. The situation unfolded like this. I stood at attention outside his office and firmly knocked three times on the "knock spot." A gravelly voice said "Enter!" I marched in, stood eighteen inches from his desk, braced at attention, and snapped a salute. The exchange of pleasantries went as follows:

Pelton: Recruit Seaman Pelton reporting as ordered, sir!

Bligh: So Pelton you want to become a line officer like me and be a boat driver is that correct?

Note: the term line officer comes from the old naval tradition when eighteenth-century warships would turn to form a line to take advantage of the cannons along the side of each ship.

Pelton: No sir. I am best qualified to serve my country and my navy as an aerographer officer.

Bligh: What the hell is that, Son?

Pelton: Sir, an aerographer is a weatherman, sir. Based upon my academic background and knowledge of the sciences, I feel it is the best way I can serve my navy and my country. Also, I am colorblind, which precludes me from being a line officer, sir.

Bligh: The Navy doesn't need any more God-damn weathermen!

The next sound in the room was a huge rubberstamp coming down on my OCS application. While I could not read the stamp, I knew that my career as a naval officer had come to a close before it had even started.

LIFE LESSON NUMBER TWO (REVISITED):
NOT EVERYTHING TURNS OUT THE WAY YOU WANT IT TO.

Author: front row, third from left

I wasn't exactly sure what was in store for me as the next step of my naval career, but I knew I had one thing going for me. At that time, there was a whole new phenomenon entering the military: computers. No one knew exactly how they worked or exactly what they did in the navy, but I did. Truth be told, I was a computer geek long before the term became commonplace.

When I was finally allowed to thaw out from my training at Great Lakes, the navy made it up to me and sent me to San Diego. Sunny skies 300 days out of the year, balmy weather, women, and beer. (Do you see a recurring theme here?) Of course this was the '70s in California, also known as the land of fruits and nuts. And when your haircut was "high and tight," it was pretty obvious who signed your paycheck.

The navy uses the term A school where they send new recruits to be trained in whatever skills the navy needs. I was detailed to the navy's computer A school. Fortunately, I was over 21, and I knew as much or more than the instructors, and I started to hang out with them more than with my student peers.

As luck would have it, one of my new instructor friends was good buddies with the detailer at BUPERS (Bureau of Naval Personnel, Washington, DC). It is the detailer at BUPERS who makes all the duty assignments after you leave A school. One day my instructor friend came to me with a very solemn look on his face and said, "I've got some very bad news for you, buddy." He had spoken to his pal in DC. He told me I was being assigned to the naval facility on the island of Adak at the end of the Alaskan Aleutian chain of islands, and I would be running the computers for a radar system guarding against nuclear attack from the Soviet Union. (Oh great! back to the Evil Empire again.) To this day I don't know if it was a true story or not, but regardless, my street smarts kicked into high gear. I simply replied, "Okay, how can I fix this?" His reply was, "Fifty bucks and a case of Johnny Walker scotch." And the only remaining question was, "Red or black?"

Weeks later, as graduation was approaching, I began to make inquiries as to the status of my negotiations. And the only response from my friend was, "If I tell you, I will have to kill you." Not very comforting, but I trusted him.

It was graduation day from A school and the command master chief had a pile of manila folders full of the orders for everyone in the graduating class. We were lined up in alphabetical order and the chief found amusement in asking every graduate where he or she wanted to go. It didn't take a rocket scientist to observe that most of the tours were sea duty.

When he got to me:

Master chief: Pelton, so where did you want to go?

I worked my way up and down the East Coast to hopefully be near my girlfriend, Andy:

Pelton: Boston, master chief.

Master chief: No.

Pelton: Newport.

Master chief: No.

Pelton: Brooklyn.

Master chief: No.

Pelton: Norfolk.

Master chief: No.

He looked at me and said: "Mister, you're going to NAVCOSSACT."

The only response I could muster was:

Pelton: Excuse me, Master Chief, what's NAVCOSSACT?

Master chief: Naval Command System Support Activity, Building 196, Washington Navy Yard, Washington, DC.

A quick glance at my instructor colleague resulted in a slight nod of the head and a sly grin, which I acknowledged with the exact same response, and I informed my graduating colleagues that there would be "a round" waiting for them on me at the enlisted men's club.

I proposed to Andy, and 10 months later we were married on another beautiful day in New England.

So I spent most of my navy career in Washington DC in a huge computer complex with tape drives that were the size of telephone booths and disc drives that were the size of washing machines (one disc drive, mind you).

And the greatest reward of my street smarts was that I could marry my college sweetheart and we could happily begin our new life together.

Will you marry me?

All that said, no one ever shared with me what my military benefits would be during my stay in the navy or as an honorably discharged veteran. I need to take some responsibility for not having researched more on my own. I am a Viet Nam-era vet and 52,221 men and women made the ultimate sacrifice while serving in Viet Nam. I was never deployed "in country," but that statistic alone should have been sufficient motivation for me to learn more about veteran's benefits. I lost some close friends during the war and I pay my respects whenever I can.

If you are a vet and would like to learn more about the benefits available to vets and their spouses, the next section is designed specifically for you.

VETERANS' BENEFITS PLANNING

"From the bitter cold winter at Valley Forge, to the mountains of Afghanistan and the deserts of Iraq, our soldiers have courageously answered when called, gone where ordered, and defended our nation with honor."

—SOLOMON ORTIZ

There are several benefits available to veterans upon their death. But I advise that you will need to do your homework and have some important information readily available.

To apply for a veteran's death benefit through the U.S. Department of Veterans Affairs (VA) you will need:

- the veteran's discharge certificate (also called the DD 214)
- the veteran's Social Security number
- a copy of the veteran's birth certificate
- the veteran's death certificate
- a copy of his/her marriage certificate if applicable
- a copy of any divorce decrees if applicable
- a copy of each child's birth certificate or adoption order

To obtain further assistance in making your claim, you can contact the VA at 1-800-827-1000 or go online to www.va.gov.

BURIAL IN VA NATIONAL CEMETERIES

Eligible veterans, their spouses, and their dependents may be buried in national cemeteries at no cost. The range of services includes the gravesite, grave liner, opening and closing the grave, and a headstone or marker.

The Veterans Administration manages 125 national cemeteries throughout the country. Some cemeteries will accommodate casket burials, while others only accept cremated remains. Usually a funeral director will be able to provide your family with some insight regarding the national cemeteries in your area. To find the one nearest you, go to: www.cem.va.gov.

Note: In most cases surviving spouses do not lose their eligibility for burial in a national cemetery should they remarry.

Veterans are eligible for an inscribed headstone or marker at their grave at no cost. The inscription includes the name of the deceased, branch of service, and dates of birth and death. Additional approved markings or words of endearment may also be added. The VA will ship a headstone anywhere in the world at no cost.

HEADSTONES OR MARKERS AT PRIVATE CEMETERIES

Headstones and markers for private cemeteries are also available at no cost through the VA.

Note: it is important to confirm the rules and regulations *of the local cemetery* regarding the approved sizes and shapes of grave markers before placing the order with the VA.

The headstone order form is VA Form 40-1330 *Application for Standard Government Headstone or Marker* which can be requested at 1-800-827-1000 or by going online at www.va.gov. The completed form should be mailed to:

Memorial Programs Service (41A1)
U.S. Department of Veterans Affairs
5109 Russell Road
Quantico, VA 22134-3903

Or the form can be faxed to 1-800-455-7143

PLOT ALLOWANCE

The VA will pay a $300 plot allowance in a private cemetery when a veteran is discharged due to a disability injury incurred or aggravated in the line of duty.

MILITARY HONORS

Upon request, the U.S. Department of Defense will provide military honors consisting of flag folding, flag presentation, and the playing of Taps. The toll free number to request this service is 1-877-MIL-HONR.

✓ HOT TIP ———————————

It is recommended that the family provide as much lead time as possible when making this request. It may be more efficient if the funeral director makes this request on behalf of the family.

A GUIDE TO BURIAL AT ARLINGTON NATIONAL CEMETERY

Eligibility for Ground Burial

Categories of those eligible for ground burial in Arlington National Cemetery, Arlington, Virginia, are specified below. However, the last period of active duty of former members of the U.S. Armed Forces must have ended honorably. Interment may be casketed or cremated remains.

a. Any active duty member of the Armed Forces (except those members serving on active duty for training only).

b. Any veteran who is retired from active military service with the Armed Forces.

c. Any veteran who is retired from the Reserves is eligible upon reaching age 60 and drawing retired pay; and who served a period of active duty (other than for training).

d. Any former member of the Armed Forces separated honorably prior to October 1, 1949, for medical reasons and who was rated at 30% or greater disabled effective on the day of discharge.

e. Any former member of the Armed Forces who has been awarded one of the following decorations:

   1. Medal of Honor
   2. Distinguished Service Cross (Navy Cross or Air Force Cross)
   3. Distinguished Service Medal
   4. Silver Star
   5. Purple Heart

f. The President of the United States or any former President of the United States.

g. Any former member of the Armed Forces who served on active duty (other than for training) and who held any of the following positions:

   1. An elected office of the U.S. Government
   2. Office of the Chief Justice of the United States or of an Associate Justice of the Supreme Court of the United States.
   3. An office listed, at the time the person held the position, in 5 USC 5312 or 5313 (Levels I and II of the Executive Schedule).
   4. The chief of a mission who was at any time during his/her tenure classified in Class I under the provisions of Chapter 411, Act of 13 August 1946, 60 Stat. 1002, as amended (22 USC 866) or as listed in State Department memorandum dated March 21, 1988.

h. Any former prisoner of war who, while a prisoner of war, served honorably in the active military, naval, or air service, whose last period of military, naval or air service terminated honorably and who died on or after November 30, 1993.

i. The spouse, widow or widower, minor child, or permanently dependent child, and certain unmarried adult children of any of the above eligible veterans.

j. The widow or widower of:

   1. A member of the Armed Forces who was lost or buried at sea or officially determined to be missing in action.
   2. A member of the Armed Forces who is interred in a U. S. military cemetery overseas that is maintained by the American Battle Monuments Commission.
   3. A member of the Armed Forces who is interred in Arlington National Cemetery as part of a group burial.

k. The surviving spouse, minor child, or permanently dependent child of any person already buried in Arlington National Cemetery.

l. The parents of a minor child, or permanently dependent child whose remains, based on the eligibility of a parent, are already buried in Arlington National Cemetery. A spouse divorced from the primary eligible, or widowed and remarried, is not eligible for interment.

m. Provided certain conditions are met, a former member of the Armed Forces may be buried in the same grave with a close relative who is already buried and the burial candidate is primary eligible.

(Source: www.ArlingtonCemetery.org/funeral_information)

✓ HOT TIP —————————————————

Burial space at Arlington National Cemetery is becoming limited and the eligibility criteria for burial at ANC may become more restricted.

CHAPTER FOUR

My Family

"My father taught me the only way you can make good at anything is to practice, and then practice some more."

—PETE ROSE

DAD

The year 1976 was a great one for our nation. It was America's bicentennial year and there were many celebrations across the country. It was also the year my dad passed away. He died of prostate cancer at age 67. To add insult to injury, he was a urologist. Dad was incredibly loyal to his practice and to his patients. He worked tirelessly until the age of 65. Then he retired. Then he died.

My dad had two primary focuses in his life: he loved his family and he loved being a doctor. But he could never truly mix the two. School plays, football games, and family time were all built around the practice of medicine. Dad was up at 5 a.m. every day, getting ready for morning rounds at the hospital, and in bed relatively early each night to get ready for the next day. That time was affectionately known as "quiet time" in our house.

And so when he was diagnosed with prostate cancer (a personal medical issue), it could not be readily shared with his children because that would make it a family issue. While I could see changes in him, such as loss of energy, loss of weight, and difficulty making decisions, the situation was not made clear to me until his cancer had reached the terminal stage. The treatments for cancers in general and prostate cancer in particular have come a long way in 35+ years, but today's treatment options were not available for my dad in 1976.

I recall one day toward the end, when my wife, Andy, and I were visiting Dad in the hospital after he had just come back from chemotherapy. He was lying there comfortably when he suddenly had a severe facial twitch, a grimace, and he let out a low moan. My immediate thought was, "Oh my God, he just died!" My next thought was a call to action. After all, I knew the drill. I'd been trained. I could resuscitate him. Move! My second immediate thought (all of this taking place in 1–2 seconds) was to stop. I knew he had a DNR note in his medical chart. DNR means "Do not resuscitate"; take no extraordinary actions to restore life. Andy and I looked at each other. She squeezed my hand, and the nonverbal body language was clear. What just happened?

✓ HOT TIP

A Do-Not-Resuscitate order is a protective order and must be written by a physician. Copies should be maintained by your physician, be available in your medical chart if you are hospitalized, and with your personal papers maintained at home.

It was now five seconds after the event and I was thinking, "Oh no! I never had a chance to truly say goodbye, let alone to express all the other thoughts I wanted to share with him before he died."

Long story short: Dad did not die that day. He just had an adverse post-chemo reaction. But I learned a critically important take-away.

✓ HOT TIP

If there are important things to be said, SAY THEM! Say them when everyone is still healthy and cognitive and say them from your heart. If there are fences to be mended, mend them. If there are records to be set straight, fix them. And if there are loving accolades to share, share them.

As often happens with family members, when a loved one is being consumed by stage IV cancer, you will suggest going to almost any lengths to find a cure. When I adamantly lobbied with Dad that he should explore going to the Mayo Clinic or the Sloan-Kettering Cancer Center, he said, "No! I want to go back home, be with my books, listen to the ducks, and eat a hot fudge sundae every day!"

I thought that dementia had taken its toll. He was a knowledge-able physician who had forgotten more about prostate cancer than I could ever hope to learn, yet he was refusing to seek help from some of the most prestigious cancer treatment centers in the country.

But you know what? He *did* know best. He did what he wanted. He did go home, and he read avidly every day, and if I had been a smart entrepreneur back then, I would have purchased the local

Friendly's Ice Cream Shoppe franchise. Dad died peacefully, at home, being serenaded by the ducks on the lagoon in our backyard.

✓ HOT TIP ————————————————

Within reason, let elderly or dying people control their own destiny and environment for as long as possible.

————————————————————

Little did I recognize it at the time, but the seed that would become *The Ultimate Family Gift* was planted back in 1976 by my loving father. However, there were more lessons to learn. Talking about death and dying is a challenge today, but it was clearly taboo back in 1976. I had no idea if Dad wanted to be cremated, or buried, or even which cemetery he preferred. Whether or not my parents ever discussed this still remains unclear, but clearly such topics were never discussed with the kids. Mom decided that it would be best if Dad were cremated and then buried in his family plot in New York State. Years later she decided that she too would like to be cremated but buried behind her church in Bay Head on the Jersey shore. A few years later I made some progress. I was able to have some heart-to-heart discussions with my mother regarding her wishes before she died. The seed to create *The Ultimate Family Gift* that was planted in 1976 when Dad passed away just got a little water and sunshine from Mom years later. As time passed, Mom decided that she would like to exhume my dad and move him to the same small church cemetery in New Jersey where she planned to be buried so they could be together when she passed away. This event was a challenge for me, but I supported her decision because it was what she wanted.

However, all of this anguish could have been eliminated if everyone had been involved from the beginning. Having the opportunity to have frank discussions about what you would like to have happen when you die is critical.

Finally, there were financial benefits available to us as the surviving family that we never knew about—or benefitted from. When Social Security beneficiaries die, the surviving family may be eligible for either a lump sum payment and/or a monthly distribution from Social Security, given certain qualifying conditions.

Read on to learn some planning tips and things to know about how the U.S. Social Security Administration works. Hopefully you can take advantage of the opportunity that was lost for my family.

SOCIAL SECURITY PLANNING

"Americans need accurate information in order to consider Social Security reform. Too bad the media can't be counted on to provide it."

—HERMAN CAIN

WILL MY FAMILY BE ABLE TO COLLECT MY DEATH BENEFITS UNDER SOCIAL SECURITY?

Let's begin with the age-old question of "Will Social Security even be around for someone to collect?" The answer is definitely yes.

Whether or not your children or even your children's children will be able to receive Social Security benefits and be paid relatively similar benefit amounts remains to be seen. That question may not be answered by the U.S. government until long after we have left the planet.

WHAT ARE YOUR DEATH BENEFITS UNDER SOCIAL SECURITY?

Under the current system, your Social Security benefits may be transferable to qualifying surviving family members. Examples include:

- a widow or widower
- a widow or widower of the deceased caring for a child who is less than 16 years old
- dependent parents who are age 62 or older
- any disabled child
- unmarried children under the age of 19
- stepchildren, grandchildren, and adopted children

The amount of benefits each dependent may receive depends on several factors that are much too numerous to share here. My suggestion is that you invest some time to visit your local Social Security office to get the full details on your particular situation.

To find the closest Social Security office near you go to: www.socialsecurity.gov

HOW DOES MY SURVIVING FAMILY APPLY FOR MY DEATH BENEFIT?

The good news is that the process is fairly simple. The bad news is that you need to dot several i's and cross several t's to file a claim. When a family member wants to file a death benefit claim, he/she needs to provide the U.S. Social Security Administration with the following data:

- claimant's name
- claimant's Social Security number
- claimant's date of birth
- claimant's place of residence
- claimant's citizenship status
- claimant's military status
- earning for the previous year and for the current year in which the claim is made
- claimant's marriage dates and status
- any previous Social Security claims
- name of the deceased
- deceased's Social Security number
- deceased's date of birth
- deceased's date of death
- deceased's location of death
- deceased's earnings from the previous year and the current year
- deceased's marriage dates and status

HOW MUCH CAN I COLLECT FROM SOCIAL SECURITY WHILE I'M STILL ALIVE?

This is a great question, and like so many questions raised in this book, there is no single answer. Factors that influence your specific benefits are related to how long you have worked, the amount of your annual income, and the age at which you start collecting your Social Security benefits.

Right now the minimum age to collect is 62. However, there is a financial advantage in waiting until what the U.S. Social Security Administration considers "full retirement age." Full retirement age used to be age 65, but now it is on a sliding scale of age 65–67 based on the year you were born. You will need to contact the U.S. Social Security Administration to determine what your "full retirement age" is.

For more information on your specific retirement age eligibility, check this internet link:

http://www.socialsecurity.gov/retire2/agereduction.htm

HOW CAN I FIND OUT WHAT I HAVE PAID INTO THE SOCIAL SECURITY SYSTEM THUS FAR?

There is a great report you can get automatically from the U.S. Social Security Administration that clearly outlines all of the Social Security taxes you have paid into the system and, based on that data, it also tells you what your projected Social Security benefits are today and into the future.

It's called simply the Social Security statement.

It is a great way to verify that your data is correct, and it is a great tool to assist you in financial planning for your retirement. You can even have it automatically sent to you every year.

✓ HOT TIP ———————————

To order your copy of the report, you can call 1-800-772-1213 and request an application for the Social Security statement (Form SSA-7004-SM) or get it online at www. socialsecurity.gov. If you want to see your information online and print your own report, go online to www. socialsecurity.gov/myaccount to set up your account.

IS THE SOCIAL SECURITY PROGRAM IN FINANCIAL TROUBLE?

The simple answer is that there is more cash flowing "out" of the system than income coming "in." When we get paid each week or biweekly, a portion of the money we all work so hard for goes into the Social Security trust fund. This amount is matched by your employer. The original goal was to have the interest earned on the trust fund investments pay for Social Security retirement benefits and Medicare program costs. Over time, the number of participants in the program (yes, all those damn baby boomers) has overloaded the system and the number of entitlement programs within the Social Security system has increased as well. The challenge is that the demands (i.e., payments) currently being paid out are consuming the available funds from the interest-bearing accounts faster than money is being generated. The financial troubles that have occurred in the past and high unemployment rates have exacerbated the strain on the system. All of those laid-off folks are no longer fueling the system with their payroll taxes. On top of that, the baby boomer crunch has started to hit the Social Security system and some serious challenges lie ahead.

The real fly in the ointment is how to fix these problems. It involves politics, making hard decisions, and asking common sense to prevail in Congress. Talking about the fixes is simple. However, finding one that will not jeopardize a politician's shot at reelection is the problem. Here are some options to address the problem:

Option One: Increase payroll taxes. The more money put into the system, the more interest it will generate. But ... that would be unpopular with everyone who works.

Option Two: Decrease the benefits that are paid out. The less money paid out, the longer the system will last. But ... that would be unpopular with all the retirees.

Option Three: Dip into the principle of the trust fund to shore up the cash going out. But ... that is just irresponsible fiscal management which has the long-term effect of simply destroying the entire system.

Option Four: Adjust the eligibility entry age from age 65 to age 67–70. But ... that will prove to be unfortunate for all the baby boomers age 65–67 who will probably share their displeasure at the voting booth.

Conclusion: There is a great deal of speculation that Social Security is doomed to failure and that there will be no money left in the system for our children and our children's children.

In my opinion, the politicians in Washington, DC, will never let Social Security die. It would be political suicide. That being said, they may poke at it, tweak it a bit, and maybe change the rules slightly. But at the end of the day it is incumbent upon each of us to track the money we have put into the Social Security system to assure that our contributions are properly recorded, and to learn what our retirement payout options are.

PETE

*"The highlight of my childhood was making my brother
laugh so hard that food came out his nose."*

—GARRISON KEILLOR

My older brother, Peter, died in 1988, and his passing was a little unique for the time. Pete was gay and lived in San Francisco. He died from complications related to HIV. Pete was a special part of my life. He was a groomsman at my wedding, and when I visited him in San Francisco, we always had a great time together. While that was only a quarter of a century ago, society's general view of the gay community back then was entirely different than it is today. To make a long story short, when Pete got extremely ill, I got a call from his partner telling us that if our family wanted to say goodbye, we needed to get on a plane ASAP. Needless to say, we all flew out the next day. When we arrived, Peter was comatose, emaciated, on life support, living without pain on a morphine drip, and taking nutrition via a nasal feeding tube. Each of us took time to share final thoughts with my brother and say goodbye. The attending physician told us that Pete would remain on life support until *we* turned it off. Peter's physician

was not authorized to discontinue life support himself. "There is nothing in the hospital chart authorizing me to do so," he told us.

We anguished over what to do. The biggest challenge was that none of us knew what Pete *wanted* us to do. By the end of the day we reached a consensus, and I turned off his life support equipment.

The discussion of living wills and creating health directives is dedicated to my brother Peter. But once again it doesn't stop there.

Being a traditionalist, my mom thought that it would be appropriate to have a full-blown funeral with all the traditional elements for Pete. This would include a wake, funeral, burial, and reception.

It took an objective outsider, a nonfamily member, to provide us with a reality check. I'll paraphrase here. The message from Pete's partner went along these lines: "With all due respect, Mrs. Pelton, I don't think all those funeral elements are needed. Here in the Castro (part of San Francisco) we are doing 3–4 memorials a week. While Peter believed in God, he was not particularly religious. I'd recommend that Peter be cremated, that we have a small reception, release some balloons, and spread his ashes along his favorite beach."

We were all dumbstruck with a deer-in-the-headlights look. We literally had no clue on how to proceed.

Note: Wouldn't it have been nice to have already had the conversation with Pete and to have gotten all the hard questions answered? We had not planned his passing, and it presented unnecessary and difficult challenges.

In the end, we elected to proceed as directed by Pete's partner. We made arrangements to have Pete cremated and the funeral director inquired about what we wanted to do with the ashes. I mentioned casually that we would be having a memorial celebration with family and friends and then spread his ashes on the beach. The funeral director adamantly disagreed and severely reprimanded me.

I was handed a copy of Environmental Protection Agency (EPA) regulation Code of Federal Regulations (Title 40, volume 12, parts 190 to 259; revised as of July 1, 1988) which strictly prohibits the disposal, placement, or burial of ashes in an open space.

I politely thanked him for pointing that out and sparing me from making an egregious error. Had I been in my class A dress uniform I probably would have saluted him. (He would have liked that part.)

With this new-found information in our hands, we proceeded directly to Lands End Beach in San Francisco and fulfilled my brother's wishes of spreading his ashes as desired. Each of us took a stone from the beach, smoothed by wind and water over eons of time. It remains one of my most precious possessions today.

✓ HOT TIP ———————————

Even in the most trying circumstances, honoring a family member or loved one needs to be compassionate, special, and permanent.

I cannot emphasize enough how much a living will or advanced health care directive could have eased the pain and anguish of Pete's passing. I am hopeful that the next section can reduce the suffering you may be experiencing now or will at some point in the future.

THE LIVING WILL

WHAT EXACTLY IS A LIVING WILL?

A living will has many names. It is also known as an advanced health care directive or a medical power of attorney. These documents allow you to state the extent of medical care wanted (or not wanted) should you become incapacitated, and to identify who is trusted to make medical decisions on your behalf.

For example, let's say you suffered a serious stroke and are in a coma. Would you like to have every medical and technological attempt made to resuscitate you or would you prefer to let nature take its course?

I shared with you my story about my brother Peter. Pete did not have a living will. Having such a document available would have made some of the challenging decisions my family had to face that much easier.

✓ HOT TIP ————————————————————

A living will is priceless in the guidance and support it can give your family. Appreciate that when it is time to exercise your living will, it's not about you. It's about your family.

————————————————————

Some folks maintain that having a living will, or advanced health care directive is even more important than having a last will and testament. With a living will, you can document your medical treatment wishes should you be incapacitated or unable to speak for yourself. Here's the big difference from a standard last will and testament: you need a living will when you are still alive.

Your living will is a binding document for use by attending physicians and the health care facilities, and it outlines the amount of treatment, intervention, and technology you desire. More importantly, you can also state when further medical treatment should be discontinued.

SO WHO IS MY HEALTH CARE AGENT?

In your living will you can assign a person to be your health care agent and this person speaks on your behalf regarding all of your health care treatment if you are incapacitated. The three key necessities in assigning your health care agent are that this person (1) is someone you trust implicitly, (2) has a clear understanding of your treatment goals in the event you cannot speak for yourself, and (3) will steadfastly maintain your requests in the face of adverse medical positions or excessive pressure from other family members.

You may want to assign two health care agent representatives in case one of them should pre-decease you. Make sure all your medical goals are in writing.

Let's try to explain it with an example. Let's say that you had the misfortune of being hit by a bus. You were in rough shape, maybe in a coma, and you were declared brain dead by all current definitions of the medical community. Your prognosis for a full recovery is nil, so what should your family do? They can elect to keep you "alive" by every modern technological means possible, or they can elect to keep you hydrated, not in pain, and let nature take its course.

Now here's the deal. The living will, or advanced health care directive, lets you control your outcome. Your final medical disposition should not be a question of what *they* want; it is the determination of what you want.

The attorney who drafts your last will and testament can also help you with your living will.

✓ HOT TIP ————————————

A copy of your living will needs to be kept with your medical chart in your physician's office and in the hospital where you are being treated. Additional copies should be available to your care givers and executor as well. Short answer: your living will needs to be immediately available while you are living.

MOM

> *"Who in their infinite wisdom decreed that Little League uniforms be white? Certainly not a mother."*
>
> —ERMA BOMBECK

Mom passed away in 1991. She was 83 and her heart simply wore out. Thankfully we had plenty of time to discuss funeral plans with her and to outline what songs and readings she wished to have at her service.

Now you can see the important changes that started to happen. Based on our past experiences, my family had the opportunity to build upon those stressful situations. We realized that having end-of-life conversations is as important to the decedent as it is to the surviving family members.

It should now be evident how the outline of *The Ultimate Family Gift* gained more traction, although the idea was still in my head at the time of my mother's funeral.

✓ HOT TIP ─────────────────

It is equally important to start the conversation for all concerned, especially the ones left behind to carry out the plan. You can't talk when you're gone!

───────────────────────────

There comes a point where you do not want to burden your will or trust with the details of all the personal property that needs to be distributed to your heirs. You may want to consider forming a personal legacy where you outline who should get which items or possessions. A personal legacy takes on more significance when numerous heirs are involved. In her final months, Mom was able to create detailed plans regarding the distribution of all of her possessions, not just the assets in her will. This became an important project to her as her final days approached. It also gave her a sense of closure. The plan gave her great comfort because she had control over the entire process, which was incredibly simple.

All the heirs gathered in Mom's house and were given a blank

legal pad. Each heir was instructed to wander the entire house and jot down any item he/she might be interested in. Each list was long and varied. An item might be as practical as the grandfather clock or as personal as a picture of "Feeding the Ducks" from years ago.

We reconvened and prioritized our wish list. Then Mom held court. There was only one rule: none of the items listed had any monetary value. The "value" was purely in the eye of the potential recipient. We went through each list, and if there were no conflicts, each heir got his/her first, second, third choice, and so on. If a possession was sought simultaneously by two heirs, Mom was the sole arbiter. Mom's rule: no discussion, no debate. Her decision was final and binding. The planning worked well, and each heir had a clear understanding of the outcome.

✓ HOT TIP ──────────────────

Most importantly Mom had complete control over the process and outcome. When people realize their days are numbered, giving them as much control as possible over their destiny is critically important.

In the best of all scenarios, you can bring the heirs together and solicit their input on which of your belongings (furniture, pictures, books, etc.) they would like to inherit after you pass away. A concise list should be compiled, outlining who gets which items.

There are four positive outcomes from this exercise.

1. You have the peace of mind that each of your chosen heirs gets something of yours that he/she truly desired.
2. The heirs have a chance to participate in the distribution of your valuables.
3. There is no question regarding who gets what items.
4. Any items left over can be donated to Goodwill, the Salvation Army, or the charity of your choice, without remorse or concern. There may even be some tax benefits to consider.

On occasion, a strange thing happens among the heirs when someone passes away. Verbal promises are not kept, and common sense and courtesy can evaporate. Even in the most harmonious, loving families, heirs are sometimes prone to struggling over a loved one's possessions. Writing things down is critically important.

✓ HOT TIP ─────────────────

A solid well-defined legacy plan both inside and outside your will or trust is a good safeguard against any disputes. Be sure to share a copy of your personal legacy list with your lawyer and executor in case a dispute should arise.

Want to learn more about building your own legacy? Read on.

BUILDING A LEGACY

"I only hope that we don't lose sight of one thing, that it was all started by a mouse."

—WALT DISNEY

Considering how you want to dispose of your assets when you die surely cannot be considered a pleasurable exercise. Creating a legacy is something you can do on your own. Once you are finished, you will work with your lawyer to build it into your will or trust.

A legacy is a gift to a person, charity, or organization that you outline in your will or trust. This donation does not go through your heirs. Simply stated, this is your opportunity to do something special for someone or some organization when they least expect it.

Ask yourself this question: If, after I have adequately protected the financial future of my surviving family through estate planning, some money or assets remain, who else would I want to help? It could be a school, agency, organization, or cause. That's what building a legacy into your will or trust is all about.

There are four types of legacies to consider:

1. Cash legacy: you leave a specific amount of money to a person or an organization.
2. Specific legacy: you leave a specific item (e.g., grandfather clock, piece of jewelry, etc.) to a person or an organization.
3. Proportionate legacy: you leave a portion of your estate to a person or an organization.
4. Residuary legacy: you leave all your estates, after all the debts of the estates have been paid off, to a person or an organization.

As you consider who might benefit from your legacy, be sure to ask your estate planner what tax benefits might be available as well.

In wrapping up this section, we have already discussed a process to distribute personal items as part of creating your own legacy. I cannot stress enough how important it is to complete this phase of end-of-life planning when you and your family members are mentally sound, cognitive, and not stressed by a death in the family.

DEB

"A few years ago, I bought an old red bicycle with the words 'Free Spirit' written across its side, which is exactly what I felt like when I rode it down the street in a tie-dyed dress."

—DREW BARRYMORE

The last member of my immediate family to die was my sister Debby, in 1998. She had ovarian cancer. She died peacefully with her family at her side. Once again, I highly recommended, from the beginning, that her family take the opportunity to discuss her funeral goals with each of us.

On more than one occasion we had a heart-to-heart discussion with all of my immediate, now-adult, family members, consisting of Deb, Deb's three children, Cindy, Jeff, and Scott, myself, Andy, Jen, and Pete's daughter, Stef.

We talked about the good times and the sad times. We talked about accomplishments and failures. We mended all the fences. We set the record straight.

And we each talked with Deb about the "gift" that she had given us. The words that came out of that conversation included love, commitment, pride, free spirit, memories, success, tenacity, affection, dedication, obliga-

Dad and Deb on her big day.

tion, humility, self-esteem and independence. Needless to say there wasn't a dry eye in the house when we were done.

✓ HOT TIP —————————————————

Have the courage to start the conversation. It is difficult for me to put into words how cathartic that discussion was. Emotional? Absolutely. Painful? At times. Humorous? When humor was right. But in the final analysis we purged ourselves (and our souls) of all the meaningless conflicts and misconceptions that often clutter family relationships. As challenging as it may be to start, rest assured that the outcome is incredibly rewarding.

Deb was a free spirit, and I often admired how she looked at the world. When she was first diagnosed with ovarian cancer, we had a lot of discussion about treatment options. She opted for a holistic approach versus the more traditional treatment methods. As I had learned from my dad, it was her call to make, and I honored her choice.

A word about hospice care. It is difficult for me to adequately share what an outstanding service that hospice care givers provide. They treat the patient and not the disease as they provide comfort as one's quality of life comes to an end. The fifth medical vital sign is pain following a patient's temperature, blood pressure, pulse, and respiratory rate. Proper pain management is the first imperative vital sign in the eyes of hospice care givers. Deb's final days were in a hospice facility established by Matt Lauer of *The Today Show.* Her care was extraordinary, compassionate, caring, and enormously supportive. Candidly I do not know how those fantastic people do it every day.

✓ HOT TIP ────────────

Medicare will fund hospice services when a physician has determined and certifies when a person has less than six months to live.

────────────────

We discussed at length what she wanted to happen when she died. Always a great organizer, she planned everything. She elected to be cremated and have a memorial service to celebrate her life. For the memorial service she wrote the program and selected the color of the paper it would be printed on, and she even picked out the ribbon that would be tied around it. The balloons were red, white, and blue. She outlined whom she wanted to speak at her service, and she also wanted to have an open forum for anyone to say some kind words. It was a great day for Deb and a great day for her family. Having a pre-planned funeral plan eliminates all the guesswork for the surviving family at a time when they are emotionally overwhelmed.

Given all of the progress that I made in planning for my family's last wishes, you may be thinking that *The Ultimate Family Gift* has come full circle, that it rose like a Phoenix from the ashes, is easily understood and its advice is simple to implement.

Not so. Now we move from my immediate family to my in-laws.

Presiding at Deb's Memorial Service

FRED AND VIRGINIA

"Humor is always based on a modicum of truth. Have
you ever heard a joke about a father-in-law?"

—DICK CLARK

My wife's parents, Fred and Virginia, were the salt of the earth. You would be hard pressed to find two folks who were more loving, caring, and supportive. They were great and they worshipped their granddaughter, Jennifer. However, the one flaw they both shared was that they were very stubborn. They belonged to the generation that survived the Depression, fought in World War II, had strong religious ties, loved the USA, and lived the American dream. They worked hard and lived in a comfortable home full of life and laughter.

However, when it came to discussing the need for a will, or funeral planning, they would have none of it. I got the feeling that they felt that discussing these subjects would shorten their lives. As their son-in-law, I always felt an undercurrent of "Thanks, but it is none of your business."

When it came to a will, they felt there was no need. With my wife, Andy, being their only daughter, they thought everything would immediately go directly to her, and would not pass through probate. When it came to discussing funeral needs, the common refrain was, "We'll discuss it later." Later never came.

They have both passed away. Fred died first, and when I approached Virginia to discuss what she thought Fred might like in terms of a funeral, my marching orders were simple: "Do whatever you think is right." Okay, so now it becomes *my* business. This was not a great deal of help to the surviving family.

When the same question was posed to Virginia on her death bed, she had the exact same response as Fred. We had made a little progress. The only comment she made was that she did not want to be cremated.

The failure of my in-laws was that they did not want to engage in even the basic discussions regarding their funerals and final wishes. For my wife, Andy, this simply made the grieving period during their passing that much tougher.

✓ HOT TIP ─────────────

Even as the objective outsider (an in-law, neighbor, friend of the family) it is okay for you to encourage or even start the challenging conversation of what funeral arrangements your friends or family members would like. After all it's not just about them, it's about all the rest of us too.

─────────────

Feeling a little overwhelmed at this point and need some additional help? I've got just the resource for you. Go to www.timpelton.com/9ways and download my free report, *Nine Ways to Start the Hardest Conversation Ever.*

My in-laws were fabulous people, but there were some serious disconnects. They survived the Depression, but they did not trust banks. They participated in the Great War, working in factories and serving in the Pacific and came home to renewed prosperity. Financial planning meant keeping everything in cash. They had the perspective that insurance salesmen were only selling insurance to get a commission and the government would take care of everything else.

There is always time to make a financial plan, but be aware the clock is running. If you need to create a financial plan with your family, the following are some things to consider.

DEVELOPING A FINANCIAL PLAN

"Banks have a new image. Now you have 'a friend,' your friendly banker. If banks are so friendly, how come they chain down the pens?"

—ALAN KING

SO WHAT HAPPENS TO ALL OF YOUR FINANCES WHEN YOU DIE?

While trying not to be too inconsiderate, the answer is: lots of things. Again, I am not providing you with legal opinions. My comments are based upon the experience of managing the deaths of my own family members, and the advice I have received from knowledgeable professionals. I highly recommend that you work with an attorney and an estate planner long before your death to help you determine (1) what is best for your family, and (2) how to minimize tax obligations on your estate upon your passing.

It would be very nice if all of your debt obligations could die when you do, but unfortunately it doesn't work that way. There are many different rules that apply and the rules can vary from state to state. So it is critically important that you plan ahead now.

WHAT ABOUT YOUR BANK ACCOUNTS?

Upon notification of your death, your bank will freeze all accounts that are solely owned by you. The cash value of those closed accounts become an asset of your estate and can only be liquidated through the probate process.

Any accounts held jointly will remain open and can be used by the cosigner(s) of the account. Obviously once you have died, you have no control over how the money in your joint bank account is managed, so plan accordingly and select your joint account holders carefully.

"Yes," you say, "but I'd like my family to manage my funeral and be able to pay for it out of *my* bank account, not to mention all the additional expenses during probate including mortgage payments, taxes, and utilities."

You have several options, all of which have pros and cons.

The first and most practical option is that most banks will release sufficient funds from a frozen account to cover the reasonable cost of a funeral. Note the operative word is *most*. Not all banks will. It's a good idea to discuss this option with your banker.

The second option is to establish a payable-on-death bank account. Under this arrangement you set aside funds in a separate bank account to pay for your funeral and related expenses. You assign a beneficiary who can immediately utilize the funds in the account upon presentation of your death certificate to the bank. This will assist your heirs in managing your affairs until the probate process can liquidate your estate.

✓ HOT TIP ─────────────────

It is extremely risky and dangerous for your heirs to deliberately fail to notify the bank of your passing and to continue to write checks against your checking account and/or make withdrawals from your savings account. That constitutes bank fraud. Consequences can include prosecution and jail time.

As an example, let's say your heirs agree to sell your home as part of the probate process which, as we know, can take a long time. So in the mean time, who will pay for the taxes, utilities, maintenance, and upkeep of the house? Answer: Your heirs will.

✓ HOT TIP ─────────────────

From the time of the posting of the probate notice, your creditors have up to one year (based on the state you reside in) to make a claim against your estate.

There are only two challenges with payable-on-death bank accounts. The first is that you can only have *one* beneficiary assigned to the account. Obviously it needs to be someone you trust to manage your funds as you desire after you die. The second is that, as tempting as it may be, you cannot place large sums of money in the account simply to avoid the probate process. The IRS does not look favorably upon such actions.

Bank accounts are a pretty good deal. While you are alive, you can make withdrawals, change beneficiaries, or even close out the account if you so desire. Once you pass away, the designated beneficiary presents your death certificate to the bank and then has access to those funds.

WHAT ABOUT A BANK SAFE DEPOSIT BOX?

A safe deposit box is a double edged sword. It is an extremely safe place in which to store your valuable and important documents. It can also be extremely hard to access, especially in times of an emergency or in the event of your death.

The laws of your state define who can and who cannot have access to your safe deposit box once you die. In some states it is relatively easy to have co-renters (another person, or other persons, authorized by you to have access to your safe deposit box, such as family members or your executor) assigned to open your safe deposit box. Other states may require a court order to do so. Check with your bank official to learn more about the banking regulations in your particular state.

Timing may be an essential issue when trying to access a safe deposit box. I mentioned that the bank will freeze all accounts upon notification of your death. This will include your safe deposit box. However, until the bank has been officially notified that you have died, the co-renter still has straight-forward access to the safe deposit box and its contents. Always choose wisely when giving co-renters access to your safe deposit box.

IS THERE AN ALTERNATIVE TO A SAFE DEPOSIT BOX?

Yes, you can use a safe at home or in your office. But once again, you need to pick wisely who has access to the combination of your safe.

One advantage to having your own safe at home is that the contents are available 24 hours a day, not just when the bank is open. Often there is also more space in a safe to store important documents, cash, and valuable jewelry.

However it should not be just any safe. Picking the right safe for your use is very important. Design considerations when selecting a safe should include:

- sufficient space, in terms of cubic feet, to store all your needs;
- an Underwriters Laboratory (UL) fire resistance rating of at least 2 hours;
- an Underwriters Laboratory (UL) burglary-tool resistance rating;
- moisture resistance;
- ability to bolt the safe to a floor or wall;
- manual access to the digital keypad if the safe has one (in case the keypad fails).

And last, but not least, always be cautious regarding who knows and has access to the safe's combination.

My personal choice is to keep all emergency-critical information in a safe in my house and keep all less mission-critical information in a safe deposit box. Keep it simple. Those items that need to be acted upon immediately go into the safe.

As an example, copies of our living wills, standard wills, important passwords, bank account numbers, credit card numbers, prepaid funeral plans, purchased cemetery plot information, and the safe deposit box key reside in the safe. Deeds, car titles, life insurance policies, and stock certificates all can go into the safe deposit box.

✓ HOT TIP

When purchasing a pre-paid funeral plan be sure to ask what will happen if you move, cancel the plan, or the funeral home or plan goes out of business.

WHAT ABOUT ALL THE CREDIT CARD ACCOUNTS I HAVE?

When you pass away, there are two methods by which the outstanding balance on your credit card account is managed. The credit card company can tell your survivors if the account was held solely or jointly.

If the credit card is held solely in your name, the debt payment obligation comes out of your estate. Your probate executor is responsible for reconciling your debts in probate court. Based on the amount of the balance due, some credit card carriers will opt to simply write off the amount due to be paid to them rather than wait for the probate process to take place.

Some credit card organizations may send collection letters to family members at the same address demanding payment of the outstanding balance. The family is not obligated to pay off the debt on a credit card held solely in the name of the deceased. Those letters need to be sent back to the credit card agency telling them to redirect their inquiry to the probate court.

If the card is held jointly, the debt immediately transfers to the other name on the credit card. It becomes that person's obligation to pay off the rest of the debt, regardless of whether that person participated in making the card charges.

✓ HOT TIP ──────────────────

The credit card agency will never know if someone passes away unless you tell them. You need to notify the credit card company immediately upon someone's death. For this reason it is a good idea to keep a list of credit cards and contact telephone numbers handy in a safe location.

Unless the credit card is held jointly, the credit card carrier will freeze the account to prevent any additional charges being made. More importantly, this step further prevents any identity theft issues and it reduces the likelihood of excessive late fees and interest accumulation due to nonpayment, should the mail go unanswered.

THE THREE MAJOR CREDIT BUREAUS SHOULD BE NOTIFIED.

Just as you want to notify the three major credit bureaus when your credit cards are stolen, you also want to notify the credit agencies when the card holder dies. This is your best protection against identity theft.

Their contact information is as follows:

TransUnion:

www.transunion.com

(800) 493-2392

Experian:

www.experian.com

(888)-397-3742

Equifax:

www.equifax.com

(888)-766-0008

CHAPTER FIVE

It's a Miracle—I

*"A dad is someone who holds you when you cry, scolds you
when you break the rules, shines with pride when you
succeed, and has faith in you even when you fail."*

—UNKNOWN

February 24, 1983, proved to be a very interesting day. Andy was eight months pregnant with our baby boy. We had just wrapped up our last Lamaze class and we were thinking about what lay ahead. It was around 11:15 at night when I heard a long "Uh Oh!" coming from the bathroom. Andy said, "I think my water just broke," and I, being the ever-compassionate, supportive husband said something like, "I doubt it honey; you're only about eight months pregnant." Once again I was incorrect.

And in a scene reminiscent of the *I Love Lucy Show* we prepared in complete panic to head to the hospital. We had no overnight bag packed; nor was our "goodie" bag ready to go. Earlier that evening our Lamaze instructor had suggested that it was time to put together items that might be helpful during labor. A change of clothes, a comb, a toothbrush, a pleasing picture, and some soothing music were all supposed to be assembled and maintained in a "goodie" bag, ready to go. Such was not the case for us.

I was, however, able to check out the performance features of our 1980 Chevy Camaro RS and I reduced the 30-minute travel time to the hospital by at least a third. Hindsight would suggest that there was really no particular need to rush; labor would go for the next 30 hours. While holding hands with my beautiful bride, I truly thought I would suffer permanent damage to my hand when she had contractions. I never knew she had that much strength. And to add insult to injury, she strongly suggested that I was the sole conspirator to blame for her current condition and the likelihood that we would ever have sex again was very remote!

I had made arrangements with our obstetrician that, if everything was going well, I would be able to birth the baby. Everything was going well and I was given the go-ahead to birth our baby. The birth remains one of the greatest moments in my life. The head

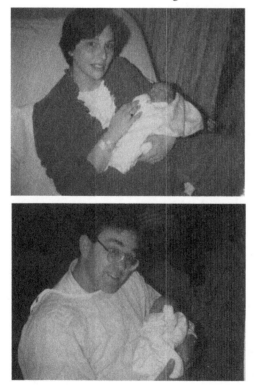

began to show—Push! Push! Rotate the shoulder —Push! Another shoulder —big push, now, one last time! Eureka—pure joy! I held this baby miracle in my two hands and I did a quick physical survey. Five tiny fingers on the right hand and five tiny ones on the left. Five really tiny toes on the right foot and five equally tiny toes on the left foot. Whoa! We are missing some very important parts. "It's a girl!" I shouted to Andy. She was in no mood for what she thought was my ridiculous and often-thought-to-be-out-of-place sense of humor. And she let me know that in no uncertain terms. I held up our bundle of joy for her viewing pleasure and we all started to cry.

It seems that there had been a misinterpretation of the ultrasound where a dangling umbilical cord seemed to strategically get in the way. Our name for the boy we thought we would have was Alexander, but that, obviously, was no longer applicable. So we considered Alexis and Jennifer, which had also been popular names way back when we were having preliminary name discussions. I conducted a quick survey of everyone in the delivery room and it was a clear vote, four to one in favor of Jennifer. It's a beautiful name for a beautiful daughter who weighed 5 pounds 7 ounces and was 15 inches long.

My mother-in-law, Virginia, who was a special person in my life, had always been a bit of a gossip, and she liked to be the center of discussions about members of her enlarged family. Once we left the delivery room and got settled in the recovery room, I called Andy's parents. Virginia answered the phone and I told her, "We had the baby and it's a girl." Her only response was, "Oh good." There was a click and she hung up the phone. She now had a tidbit of information she was bursting to tell the world about. Breaking news on CNN could not hold a candle to Virginia's need to share news. I often chuckle when I think how the dialogue must have gone with her friends and family. This was before the Internet, e-mail, and cell phones, and all the phone calls had to be made individually, and I suspect they went something like this:

Andrea had the baby and it's a girl.

Is she okay?

I don't know.

Is the baby okay?

I don't know.

What's the baby's name?

I don't know.

How big?

I don't know

When are they coming home?

I don't know?

Remember that this is back in the early 80s, and Virginia had no way of contacting us directly in the recovery room. She had to sit and wait for us to call her back to get all the pertinent information before sharing it with the world. At the end of the day we were all fine. Jennifer was tiny, but perfect. Andy finally relaxed and was on the mend. And I had my right hand on an ice pack to keep the swelling down.

Throughout her entire pregnancy, Andy did an extraordinary job of being extremely careful about what she ate and drank. Food, salt, and other nutrition were all taken in moderation. While only a social drinker, she didn't drink any alcohol during the pregnancy and she was never a smoker. Cutting out the caffeine from coffee was a challenge, but what she missed most was chocolate—a struggle that I can wholeheartedly understand. In the joy of decompression from our blessed event, Andy said she would really like a big hot fudge sundae, her favorite treat. And at that point I would've been happy to get her the moon if she had she suggested it. I went out and got her a hot fudge sundae, and it is almost humanly impossible to calculate how rapidly that ice cream sundae was consumed. I heard a momentary slurping, sucking sound and it was gone! It was a scene right out of the movie *Jaws*. But the smile of satisfaction on my beautiful wife's now maternal face was priceless.

Jen is all grown up now and off on her own, but that very special day in February in 1983 will always remain the high point of my life, and she will always be daddy's little girl.

I really did not think very much about life insurance until Jen came along. Wow! Now I was a father with greater responsibilities and I began to ponder the "what if" scenario. What if I died? Would there be enough financial resources to pay off the house, pay for a college education, and provide a reasonable nest egg for the future? One way to address those concerns is to buy life insurance. Once again, it's not about you, it is all about your surviving family.

While often perceived as convoluted and confusing, purchasing life insurance does not have to be. Read on.

LIFE INSURANCE PLANNING

"There are worse things in life than death. Have you ever spent an evening with an insurance salesman?

—WOODY ALLEN

Life insurance is one of those planning elements that are often misunderstood because they have the potential to be very convoluted if you fail to ask yourself good questions regarding your needs.

Again, I am more than willing to share my insight, but I am not a knowledgeable insurance agent, nor do I claim to be. However, I strongly recommend that you work with an insurance agent who listens to your needs, and with whom you are comfortable working.

I also believe in the K-I-S-S (Keep it simple stupid) model.

WHAT QUESTIONS SHOULD I ASK THE AGENT?

Ironically, it is not a question of what you should ask the agent; it is what you need to tell him/her. You need to explain your needs and what financial support you envision your family will need after you are gone.

First question: Does anyone depend on me for financial support?

Support can be defined both in the short term and long term. Short-term support may entail paying the mortgage, paying the utility bills, and covering day-to-day expenses. Examples of long-term expenses include paying for a college education, funding a future wedding, or covering elder care needs.

If you answered no to this question, you probably do not need life insurance. If the answer is yes, you need to ask yourself (1) how many of my dependents will I need to financially support, (2) how much will they need, and (3) how long will they need it?

SO HOW MUCH WILL MY DEPENDENTS NEED?

The actual amount of insurance coverage you need is best discussed with an insurance agent, but here are some simple rules of thumb for determining how much insurance coverage you may need.

Questions to ask yourself:

- How much of the family income do I provide?
- How will my spouse, partner, and children get by when I die?

- What are the big-ticket financial obligations (mortgage, college, alimony, etc.) that will occur in the future?
- Does anyone else (parent, brother, sister, etc.) depend on me for financial assistance?
- How long should I plan to cover their needs after I'm gone?

FORMULA NUMBER ONE:

The amount of life insurance needed = Your survivors' annual expenses times the number of years they need it minus the total inheritance they will receive.

FORMULA NUMBER TWO
(REMEMBER THE K-I-S-S MODEL.)

Simply calculate your annual salary times 20.

These calculations are simply a benchmark to start the planning process. Obviously, your life insurance needs will be different if you are 30 years old and have a mortgage and two kids who will go to college, versus a 65-year-old who is about to retire and has become an empty-nester. There are lots of valuable planning tools available on the Internet. I suggest you look at 2–3 sources and compare answers.

SO WHAT KIND OF INSURANCE
POLICY DO I NEED?

There are two basic types of life insurance, and each type has pros and cons. There are also numerous combinations of the two, but for right now let's keep it simple.

TERM LIFE INSURANCE

As the name implies, term life insurance provides coverage for a specific period of time, usually 1, 5, 10, or 15 or more years. For the duration of the policy, you pay a fixed annual premium over the term of the policy. There will be a payout of the fully insured amount of the policy to your beneficiary, but only upon your death.

Pros: Term life insurance is pretty simple to understand. It is relatively inexpensive, and you have a fixed annual cost over the life of the policy.

Cons: If you do not die during the term of the policy, your "investment" has not paid off and no money is given back to you in return. However, for that same time period, you had the peace of mind that you did the right thing to attempt to protect your family.

At the end of each term, the policy needs to be renewed and may require a health history review and/or physical examination. However, there is no obligation for the insurance carrier to renew the policy. It is highly likely that the new policy will also come with a higher premium. Term life insurance policies do not have, or build, cash value.

PERMANENT INSURANCE/ WHOLE LIFE INSURANCE

This type of policy provides insurance coverage throughout the policy holder's life time as long as the annual premiums are paid. Generally the annual premiums remain at the same rate as well.

One of the unique aspects of most permanent insurance policies is that they build cash value over time. That is to say, the policy creates additional dividends that add value to the insurance policy and may even be taken out as a loan against the policy, if the policy allows for it.

Pros: The policy holder is covered for all of his or her life without the need to renew the policy, and the policy creates a cash value (i.e., savings) account that can be used in future years.

Cons: This type of policy is more expensive than term life insurance.

✓ HOT TIP ───────────────

Do not make your estate the beneficiary of your life insurance policy. Your beneficiary needs to be a person or a specific trust. Your beneficiary will receive all of the proceeds from your insurance policy tax free. If the payout goes to your estate, estate taxes will need to be paid on the amount received.

WHAT ABOUT PROBATE NEEDS AND ESTATE TAXES?

Now you have crossed the line to where you must get an estate planning professional involved. The tax laws, rules, and regulations are so convoluted that people make a career out of simply translating them into English.

Also, you might want to discuss with your insurance agent the idea of looking at a "second-to-die" permanent life insurance policy. Under this type of policy, usually covering both a husband and wife, when the first partner passes away, there is no death benefit payout of the policy. Only when the second spouse dies does the death benefit for both people get paid to the beneficiary.

The purpose of this policy is to provide a significant inflow of cash, which may be needed to fund estate taxes as the estate is liquidated.

If you are feeling a little overwhelmed, don't be. Do your homework, find an insurance agent you trust, and sleep better at night knowing you have fulfilled another task in protecting your family once you have died.

P.S. If relevant to your situation, remember to ask your benefits administrator at work if a term life insurance policy is part of your benefits package. These policies are often overlooked and/or forgotten about since the employer often pays the full premium through the business employee benefit program.

CHAPTER SIX

The Brotherhood

"My heroes are those who risk their lives every day to protect our world and make it a better place: police, firefighters, and members of our armed services."

—**SIDNEY SHELDON**

A common term used among emergency services is the brotherhood. Whether you're a firefighter, police officer, paramedic, or EMT, you develop a common bond with your brotherhood brothers and sisters as you go repeatedly into harm's way. Rarely do we think about death unless it is thrust upon us, because we truly believe "it will always be the other guy."

But sometimes the other guy is one of your own. The first loss of one of my brothers during my fire department

The Brotherhood. Author is to the right of the dalmation.

career was due to a suicide. When I was called to the scene by the police department, all that I was told was that one of my fire department colleagues had attempted suicide. As I was driving to the scene I had no sense that it was a fatal attempt.

Many times people will attempt suicide as a cry for help. An example is when someone swallows a bottle of sleeping pills but immediately calls 911 for help. Such was not the case here. It was a self-inflicted gunshot wound that was instantly fatal. Thus began my entry into the field of critical incident stress management (CISM).

The direct impact of the suicide made my fire department almost dysfunctional. We were all overwhelmed, sad, mad, and suffering from bouts of survivor's guilt. Survivor's guilt occurs when those left behind think there was something else they could have done, or some interim measure that they could have taken that might have changed a fatal outcome.

Many of us within the fire department knew parts of our deceased colleague's story. There were financial troubles, girlfriend troubles, troubles at home, and also troubles at work. But none of us knew the complete picture; we knew only pieces of the puzzle.

At that time I had some basic information about CISM teams that were available to emergency service personnel to help them process challenging and untimely events, including the death of a colleague. A local CISM team did come to the fire department and they did help us get back in service. They helped us to attempt to place this agonizing event in perspective. The session did help us to talk about the event and get the fire department back on track.

The outcome of the fire department group discussions was groundbreaking for me. People I barely knew existed came in a heartbeat, late at night, and "fixed" me and my fire department. My goal was to immediately learn more and pay it forward. I needed to learn more about CISM to be able to respond effectively to other brothers and sisters in the brotherhood when these extremely good people had an extremely bad day.

Back in the 1980s and 1990s the standard practice in emergency services was for personnel to self-medicate at a local bar after a tough call and to talk of the tragic incident only in global terms. This was euphemistically called going to "choir practice." It numbed the pain for a while, but it did little to fix the problem long term.

Now it is important to remember that back then police officers and firefighters were respected superheroes (and some had egos to match). So to be asked to talk about how you were personally impacted by a call or to talk about why you were upset would clearly violate the superman image that many emergency service personnel had of themselves.

During these early years the CISM movement within emergency services was still in its infancy. Candidly, there was an initial stigma to be overcome. There was a perception that CISM was psycho-therapy and not peer group counseling, and no emergency service personnel worth their salt would want to "sit down with a shrink!" But I immediately saw the positive impact that CISM had on me, my colleagues, and my fire department. I knew that this was something in which I needed to become more involved. I took a number of courses sponsored by the American (now International) Critical Incident Stress Foundation based in Baltimore, and I joined the same CISM team that had helped out my department. Since then I have responded to countless requests for assistance and have been pleased to pay back the system many times over. I am a strong believer that the CISM saves careers, saves families, and saves lives. It has rein-forced my view of how fragile life can be and how unpredictable the nature of dying can be.

CHAPTER SEVEN

It's a Miracle—II

"There are two ways to live: you can live as if nothing is a miracle; you can live as if everything is a miracle."

—ALBERT EINSTEIN

It's April 1984. We've been happily married for 13 years and my beautiful daughter Jennifer is one year old. My wife, Andy, and I thought about taking a long weekend alone for some quality time away together, leaving Jen with her grandparents. We needed a break and time to talk about the future. Little did we know what was going to transpire.

We opted for a long weekend in Bermuda. It was a relatively short flight from New England and we wanted to go somewhere special. As you fly into the airport in Bermuda, the views are absolutely breathtaking and soothing. The varying depths of the reefs around Bermuda and the crystal-clear waters turn the sea into a collage of beautiful blue, jade, turquoise, emerald, and aquamarine hues. The people in Bermuda are incredibly polite and thoughtful. When they say, "have a delightful day," it is not simply a saying; they truly mean that they want you to have a fantastic day on their beautiful island.

Now April in Bermuda isn't what you'd call beach weather. But coming from the cold doldrums of melting snow in Connecticut and the relentless winds of March, Bermuda was a paradise. To simply walk barefoot on beaches made of pink sand with the consistency of baby powder was a treat. Bermuda was absolutely fantastic and we have subsequently returned many times since.

On our journey home we had a connecting flight that went through Charlotte, North Carolina. With typical British colony efficiency, flights arriving in Bermuda from the USA all arrive in the morning and flights departing from Bermuda all leave in the afternoon. As we began our ascent from Bermuda, I had the luxury of looking out my window seat and observing once again the beautiful aquamarine colors below.

About 20 minutes after takeoff, we continued to ascend and were climbing above 20,000 feet. I noticed through the window that the orientation of the sun was beginning to shift. Candidly, I didn't give it much thought until I realized that the light of the sun was now coming in the windows on the other side of the aircraft. It appeared that we had made a slow turn and were now heading east instead of west. More disconcerting was the fact that the ocean appeared to be getting closer versus falling further away. And then the captain came on the public announcement system and said, "We have a report that an incendiary device may be on board and we are returning to Bermuda!"

From my years in the fire service I instantly knew that the term incendiary device was an often used euphemism for a bomb. Andy and I held each other tightly and we had one single thought in our heads: What will happen to Jennifer?

Our descent continued to about 5,000 feet above the water and it was obvious to me that the pilot had elected to explore the acceleration potential of the aircraft. As we roared over the reefs, they lost all their soothing characteristics and colors. The more vibrant colors were now the fire apparatus and ambulances staged on the airport runway with all their lights activated; they were ready to go.

In the aviation vernacular we came in hot. We ran the entire length of the runway and the pilot used full power on the jet engine reverse thrusters and hydraulic braking system to bring the aircraft to an abrupt halt as our bodies strained against our seatbelts. We had been briefed and the rules were clear: Exit the aircraft immediately. Do not bring any carryon bags, parcels, miscellaneous clothing or items in your hands. Simply get off the plane now! The only thing that we were required to have on us was our passport. The plane didn't even taxi. We deplaned where the plane had stopped and were quickly hustled down a set of old-style mobile stairs that rolled up to the aircraft door.

We were escorted down an unused runway back to the terminal. My initial reaction was that these police officers and airport officials were there to assist us in typical Bermudian polite fashion. I realized later that the "escort service" was really part of a security and investigation detail. We were all sequestered in a secure part of the terminal and no one was allowed to leave. Our passports and credentials were reviewed time and time again. The standard protocol was to allow no one back on the plane until two hours after its scheduled arrival time at its next destination. On this particular flight it was due to arrive in Charlotte, North Carolina, at 4:30 p.m. eastern standard time, which meant that closer examination of the aircraft would not begin until 7:30 p.m. Bermuda time. The plane had been towed to the farthest point from the terminal in an attempt to protect the terminal and any other aircraft on the ground if there were a detonation.

Around 9 p.m. we got the word that the plane had been searched by the bomb squad and bomb detection canines and nothing had been found. The next step entailed having all the luggage removed from the aircraft and hand-searched. Again nothing was found. At midnight, word came down that we were to go find our luggage, re-board the plane, and continue our flight home.

Again Andy and I had a unified and solitary response: "Not a chance!"

Somewhere in Bermuda at midnight there must be a hotel room. When we let the officials know that it was our intention not to board the aircraft, we became the focus of much discussions by many officials. They wanted to know why we were refusing to re-board the aircraft after it had gone through such a high scrutiny and inspection and no incendiary devices had been found. For reasons that aren't entirely clear to me, the logic that Andy and I had just "dodged a bullet" and didn't want to risk it again seemed perplexing to many officials. We were committed to staying in Bermuda, regardless of cost and as long as necessary to catch another outbound flight. We adamantly refused to get back on the original plane.

To make a long story short, we were able to get two seats on a plane the next day and had an uneventful but unnerving flight home.

While the initial goal of our weekend away was to look at our

future together, little did we know we would have a reality check that changed our lives forever. At that time our existing will and testament was an old one from my days in the navy. When the will had been drawn up, we had no real assets and no daughter. We had no affirmative action plan for what would happen to Jen if the worst happened to us, nor did we have any financial reserves set aside to protect her.

The important take-away from that special weekend was not the fact that couples need to have some quality time together to support and enhance their relationship. The harsh reality is that none of us really knows when we are going to die, and that important life lesson is never far from my thoughts and Andy's thoughts every day. It is one of the core tenets of this book.

A key element in planning for the future is a will. Your will is not a "once-and-done" document. It should be reviewed and revised as major events in your life occur and/or every five years, whichever comes first. Want to learn more about wills? Read on.

CREATING WILLS AND RELATED DOCUMENTS

"It is better to create than to learn! Creating is the essence of life."

—Julius Caesar

First and foremost, it is important to understand that I am not an attorney. Nor am I a licensed financial or estate planner. However, I have worked with a number of attorneys and estate planners whose professional opinion, knowledge, and experience I recognize and appreciate. They provided guidance on the content of this book, corroborating the accuracy of the information I want to share with you.

WHY ARE THESE DOCUMENTS IMPORTANT?

A will is a very important document to prepare. It's a no-brainer. Do it!

Here's the issue. If you have not prepared a will and you die, you have given up the opportunity to control where your assets should go.

So if I die without a will, doesn't everything still go to my spouse and/or my children?

Maybe.

If you die without a will, you have died intestate. Your estate is divided according to intestate law. Your family does not have a say in deciding who gets what. Your spouse may get some assets if they have been held jointly. If they have been held separately, a portion may go to your spouse and a portion may be distributed among those you want them to go to. But do not doubt that the government will step in to manage the situation, and we all know "the government is here to help."

Do not give up that control. Prepare a will.

OKAY, SO WHERE DO I GET A WILL?

There is a lot of free information regarding wills that you can download from the web, but you need to be diligent in your research. Creating a will is a classic example of getting what you pay for. Invest in having a will prepared by an attorney. There are legal issues to be addressed; probate needs to be discussed; estate planning goals need to be determined; and, of course, the IRS needs to be dealt with. Let an attorney coach you through the minefield of preparing a will. You'll be glad you did. Every state is different, and if you hold property in multiple states, things can get complicated quickly.

WHAT IF YOU ARE NOT QUITE SURE HOW TO GET STARTED?

We all know that the Internet holds a wealth of valuable information, but it can also serve as a minefield of bad information. There are several Internet links that may be worth checking out. Please note that I do not receive any compensation or other rewards for recommending these sites, and I encourage you to proceed with caution. Here are the links:

www.askthelawyers.com

www.onlinelawyersource.com

www.findlaw.com

www.legalzoom.com

You have spent your lifetime working hard and creating assets. You need to assure yourself that those assets will be distributed in accordance with your wishes. A will assures your achievement of this goal.

WHAT ELSE CAN AN ATTORNEY DO FOR ME?

Your lawyer can also help you draft a written power of attorney (POA) if you need one. Typically, with a POA, you are authorizing someone else to act on your behalf on a business matter.

Let's say you have moved and are living in Florida to enjoy a well-deserved retirement, but you haven't yet sold your house up North due to depressed real estate prices. You can assign a POA (a lawyer, family member, trusted friend) to act on your behalf at the real estate closing once you are able to sell the property. The POA will be very helpful if you do not want the expense and inconvenience of flying back for the closing.

Again, let your attorney create all the documents that you need. POAs should only be awarded to people you trust the most to execute your instructions.

These are the top-ten questions to ask your attorney as you get started:

1. How do you charge for your services, fixed fee or hourly rate?
2. How long will my documents take to prepare?
3. What issues may make my situation unique?
4. Will I be dealing directly with you or another member of the firm?
5. How much of your business deals with wills and estate planning?
6. Is there a fee if I choose you to be the executor of my will?
7. Have any of the wills or estate documents you've drafted been challenged in court?
8. Have any of the wills or estate documents you've drafted been challenged by the IRS?
9. How do you resolve disputes among the surviving heirs?
10. Tell me about the worst case you have ever had to deal with and how you resolved it.

 HOT TIP ———————————————

Three ways to avoid probate include having beneficiaries on insurance policies and retirement plans; assigning joint ownership on personal property (homes, automobiles, etc.); and establishing trusts where your assets automatically pass to your designated beneficiary upon your death. A

word of caution, should your desired beneficiary change over time, be sure to update the paperwork.

Make/update your will. Do it now!

CHAPTER EIGHT

Batman and Robin

"You don't know what people are really like
until they're under a lot of stress."

—TIM ALLEN

As I have mentioned earlier, my fire department was devastated by the suicide of one of our own. A CISM team came and helped us restart group discussions, gather accurate information, and establish a recovery plan. I was compelled to "pay it forward."

A key factor in CISM work is confidentiality. When conducting a proper CISM debriefing, no notes are taken and no reports are made. It is mission critical that what is said during the debriefing stays within the debriefing. I want to share with you more of my experience in dealing with the deaths of others during my CISM deployments, while not violating the sacred covenant of confidentiality.

There are several key elements in conducting a critical incident stress debriefing. The first, as I mentioned, is confidentiality. The second is to have specially trained CISM personnel, including supportive peers and a mental health professional, at every session. The peer-to-peer element is the key. Firefighters support firefighters, police support police, and paramedics support paramedics. The sessions themselves may have the appearance of a roundtable chat, but in reality they are based on a series of structured questions that encourage discussion by all participants. The discussion flows systematically, from an analysis of the facts to providing an opportunity to ventilate, from confirmation that the emotions are a normal reaction to an abnormal event to providing a roadmap outlining recovery as a process, not an event.

As the CISM movement was beginning to gain traction in 1980, I had the good fortune to meet Guy, a gentleman who was a member of the Northeast Critical Incident Stress Management response team. Guy was also heavily involved with the International Critical Incident Stress Foundation in Baltimore, and when we became partners, everything just seemed to click into place.

We enjoyed that unique phenomenon of always being in each other's head when we worked together. If one of us began a sentence, the other could finish it. We were soon known within the team as the go-to guys, anywhere, anyplace, anytime. We were labeled Batman and Robin, and it stuck. Whether it is a murder-suicide on Thanksgiving Day or a CISM response to a blizzard, the team knew that Batman and Robin were ready to go.

Guy's business ventures have since taken him around the world,

 but he remains to this day one of my closest and dearest friends.

Batman and Robin following 9/11.

YOUR TURN

By now you may be wondering what this CISM activity is all about and why it is so important. A quick example may prove enlightening. Think back to when you were 10 years old and you fell out of a tree or had a bike accident or tripped down the stairs. Take a second and think about an incident that happened to you.

Got it? Great.

Based upon how old you are, I'll bet you haven't thought of that incident in the past 20, 30, or 40 years, and yet it came out of your mental-health file cabinet in two seconds. Back then, that event was simply called a big boo-boo, but today we call it a critical stress incident. Now, the incident that you just recalled was a long time ago. I suspect that most of you have long since healed from such incidents. But with a little more thought you might be able to recall where you were, the weather that day, what you were wearing, or who helped you out.

The rationale for this is pretty simple. When we experience an extremely stressful event, specific things happen to us physiologically over which we have no control. There is a chemical dump of adrenalin and endorphins into our bloodstream. Our blood pressure goes up, as does our respiratory function. All of our senses go on high alert and our muscles tense as a neurological byproduct of our fight-or-flight syndrome through our sympathetic nervous system. The end result is that extremely stressful events provide us with a vivid memory.

Unfortunately, those of us in the emergency services often suffer the byproducts of being put in stressful situations; we often see the underbelly of our society and tragic events that are fatal. Now, for most people, that might happen once or twice in a lifetime. For emergency services personnel, those situations can easily occur once or twice a month throughout a career of 20 to 30 years. That's a lot of incidents to store in one's mental-health file cabinet.

What CISM attempts to do is "park" those significant incidents in an appropriate manner within one's psyche.

Note: The operative word is *park*, not eliminate. Tragic events are indelibly etched in your mind, and just as you are able to recall an unpleasant incident that happened when you were 10 years old, you cannot make that memory go away. However, systematically and strategically "parking" events in the mind helps emergency service personnel to achieve several goals including preserving their health, continuing their critically important duties, and saving their career.

Back to Batman and Robin.

SCHOOL SHOOTING

One of our deployments involved a shooting in a school. Obviously, for all of us, it is a challenge to understand why a young adult would opt to shoot and murder his fellow classmates.

In this case, two boys, aged 11 and 13, set up an ambush-style attack at their school. One of the boys pulled the fire alarm, and while the school was being evacuated, he and his buddy opened fire, killing four young girls and an English teacher who tried to protect her students. Ten additional children, all girls, were wounded during the violence. While these two boys had a history of disciplinary problems in the school, it is suspected that the immediate cause of the tragedy was the fact that their girlfriends had broken off their relationships with these boys.

One of a CISM response team's challenges is answering the question of why the event occurred. People look for an answer based on a reason. Unfortunately, answering such a question is not the purpose of a CISM debriefing. In the case of the school shooting, we were not able to, nor did we try to, find a satisfactory rationale for an irrational event.

THE LONGEST WALK

The single most difficult duty that emergency services personnel have to carry out is to notify family members of a relative's death. In the course of my fire service career four members of my fire department have died. None died in the line of duty. They died during emergencies to which the fire department responded only to discover the victim was one of its own, and all attempts at resuscitation were unsuccessful. One death was a suicide, another was an automobile accident, and two were industrial-type accidents.

As the department safety officer and a mental health specialist specializing in emergency service CISM, I was sometimes called upon to notify my fellow firefighters' families of their loved one's death. The walk to the front door is the longest walk you will ever have, and I tip my hat to my law enforcement and military colleagues who are called upon to perform this important function much more frequently than I.

It's critically important to get the story straight before knocking on the door because you have less than a second to deliver it. Do not stutter; do not mince words. When you knock on people's doors at 2 a.m., they know why you're there. You don't have to tell them. There is only one question in their eyes and that is whether or not their loved one is dead or alive.

One of the hardest challenges that I ever faced was being called upon to notify the wife and daughter of the death of a close firefighter and friend. Pete had died in an accident at work. Not only was Pete a colleague, but he was also a close friend. His wife was the secretary for the fire department. Once I had notified Pete's wife, I needed to find out from her where I could find their daughter, who was the same age as my daughter, Jennifer. They had grown up together. Cindy was in her first year in college. As I drove to the college campus looking for Cindy, I thought about how Jennifer would feel if she received a similar message about me. It made me pretty uncomfortable. I got the attention of her professor, who came out into the hallway. I told him that I needed to speak to Cindy. She stepped out into the hallway and she knew. Her only words were, "Is he…?"

I can remember my words exactly. "Cindy, there was an accident at work and Pete has died as a result of his injuries." And again that might have taken less than two seconds to say, but it felt as if it had taken forever. There were sobs and tears, and there were passionate hugs, and once again there was the inevitable question that I was unable to answer: why?

In another case, a motor vehicle accident involved a close fire department friend. Our fire department was dispatched to the accident location where someone was trapped. The dispatcher's voice was paced and precise. "MVA [motor vehicle accident] with entrapment. Extrication required. Time out 0246." We expedited our response.

As soon as we arrived, we immediately recognized the car involved. One of the strongest firefighters I know came to me with a tear in his eye and said, "It's him!" and simply shook his head sideways. Upon the paramedic's confirmation that the victim had died, I immediately secured all fire department operations, returning all firefighting apparatus and personnel to the closest firehouse.

Actual extrication of the body from the car would be performed by a neighboring fire department brought in by special request. Then, preserving the highest traditions of the fire service, the dead man's body was removed from the scene by members of his own fire department and his crew on Engine 2.

TWA FLIGHT 800

July 17, 1996, was a beautiful, hot, and sunny summer day without a cloud in the sky. Early that evening 230 people boarded a Boeing 747 on TWA Flight 800 headed from New York to Paris. At 8:01 p.m. Flight 800 took off from JFK airport and at 8:31 p.m. the aircraft suffered a catastrophic structural failure at 13,852 feet. The aircraft crashed into the Atlantic Ocean approximately 10 miles south of Long Island near the East Moriches Coast Guard station.

My CISM partner, Guy, had done some preliminary training with the U.S. Coast Guard District 1 CISM team based in Boston. He had also done some training with the Air Line Pilots Association (ALPA), and soon after the TWA accident he was contacted by both agencies. In the dark, early-morning hours of July 18, Guy and I were en route to Long Island. Upon our arrival at the U.S. Coast Guard station, we were tasked by the base commander to establish a CISM command post and to establish an action plan with other U.S. Coast Guard-trained CISM personnel who would be arriving later from around the country. Providing support to the U.S. Coast Guard CISM staff and the responding U.S. Coast Guard personnel would be among the most challenging and rewarding of many assignments Guy and I carried out together.

I am not very good with names in general. However, in a crisis you meet people who only pass through your life for a moment but still leave an indelible mark. U.S. Coast Guard CISM personnel Christine, Terry, Pat, Jim, and especially a navy chaplain nicknamed

Guy: top row, right.
Author: top row, third from right.

Chaps are, very simply, incredible people. Their concern and compassion for each other's well-being and their concern for their "Coastie" shipmates was a wonder to behold.

It's important to note that the primary mission of the U.S. Coast Guard is rescue. It became immediately apparent to all the U.S. Coast Guard responders that, in this case, rescue was not an option. The U.S. Coast Guard's primary responsibility would be recovery of bodies and aircraft debris. While it is obvious that the fall of an aircraft from a height of nearly 14,000 feet affords little-to-no-chance of survival, there was still universal hope among the U.S. Coast Guard personnel that they would find at least one survivor. Such would not be the case.

When a mental-health diffusing briefing is held, it is preferably done in a group setting, in a private and quiet environment. The group works through a number of structured questions, and the discussion is directed toward helping emergency responders process a tragedy without becoming overwhelmed. Again such was not the case with TWA 800.

In the first 24 hours nearly 100 victims were recovered. Based on the nature of resources immediately available, U.S. Coast Guard Group Moriches Station and Station Shinnecock search and rescue detachments (SARDET) transported the victims' remains in patrol boats to the U.S. Coast Guard pier at the Group Moriches Station. Many victims were initially recovered using smaller inflatable Zodiac boats and then transferred and staged on larger U.S. Coast Guard cutters awaiting transport to shore.

The scene was chaotic, but it was a controlled chaos. As challenging as it was, the U.S. Coast Guard personnel knew the mission before them and fulfilled that mission with extreme dedication. Latex gloves, face masks, body bags, biohazard bags, and white Tyvek protection suits were soon in short supply. Vicks VapoRub became a popular commodity to place a dab under one's nose to overcome the smell of remains and jet fuel.

Early in the recovery effort there was no opportunity to discuss all the topics encompassing a CISM health strategy with all the U.S. Coast Guard personnel involved. There was no time for group dynamics, there was no quiet environment to discuss recovery effort, and there was no time to go through a series of structured questions. The best we could do in the first 48 hours was to provide emotional support for each individual. As the boat crew members logged in their evidence, we would encourage them to get something to eat, hydrate, take additional water back out with them, call home, and sit for five minutes before they headed out again. And this went on for days.

As if the recovery of victims and debris from a major aircraft accident was not stressful enough, soon the U.S. Coast Guard command staff and U.S. Coast Guard personnel had to protect themselves from getting sucked into the black hole of a federal agency dogfight. Initially, the investigation of the aircraft accident was to be led by the National Transportation Safety Board (NTSB). That effort was managed by the NTSB vice chairman. The politics began to get a little dicey when the FBI assistant director began to get involved. The conflict was brought about by the fact that if the aircraft had been brought down by a bomb or other incendiary device, it would be up to the FBI to lead the investigation. The FBI undertook an extensive analysis to attempt to verify that specific possibility.

One of the core characteristics of any organization is unity of command: one boss and a single focus of command. The challenge with TWA 800 was determining who the boss was. Was it the NTSB or the FBI? Which organization was responsible for providing resources? With whom did rescue personnel develop short and long-range strategies? There were some very interesting staff meetings with these two federal powerhouses as they tried to work out their differences (and I am being very polite) and determine whether the NTSB or the FBI was the lead agency. When a U.S. Coast Guard boat crew brought in remains or debris to be logged in, they simply wanted to preserve the chain of evidence and not get into an Olympic urination contest over which agency to report to.

At the end of the day our CISM team had one mission and one mission only. That was to take care of the U.S. Coast Guard personnel and any other emergency responders who requested our assistance. As previously mentioned, it was a challenge to get emergency responders to sit and talk even for a moment when they were so focused on their mission. The solution we came up with was food, not much food because the Red Cross handled meals, but rather, snacks. Our base of operations was the dispensary at the U.S. Coast Guard station and we set up a snack bar where people could come and get an energy bar, a candy bar, a pack of gum, other snacks, or a bottle of water. Quite simply, we were able to buttonhook U.S. Coast Guard personnel while they were renewing supplies and grabbing a snack, do a quick mental-health check, and encourage them to take care of themselves and their shipmates.

Over time, more military assets arrived on the scene and the frantic pace of the U.S. Coast Guard personnel slow downed a bit. We could be more assertive with our CISM message, and we began to have a restorative impact on the mental health of the responders. Following a tragic situation, mental health recovery is a process, not an event. It takes time. One of the primary missions became to save careers. We had a lot of frustrated feedback from U.S. Coast Guard personnel such as, "This is not what I signed up for!" or "I joined the Coast Guard to save people!"

On day seven of the recovery, I was deployed to one of the U.S. Coast Guard cutters operating offshore. It was a long and bumpy ride in a small patrol boat. I met the crew in the galley, and I was able to conduct a diffusing briefing to get a sense of how the crew was doing. I was able to assure them that their thinking was perfectly normal for this significantly abnormal event. I told them how much their hard work meant to the surviving families and how to best take care of themselves. I also provided them with a roadmap of how their recovery would progress in the weeks to come.

All through the session I watched a senior chief gnawing on his unlit cigar. I thought he was going to eat it lock, stock, and barrel before I finished. When the session concluded and we had a little downtime, I wandered over to the chief on the pretext of making small talk, but my real intent was to discover if he had any significant mental health issues, since he was showing some preliminary symptoms.

Having dealt with old curmudgeon fire chiefs for years in similar situations, I fully anticipated that the senior chief was going to emphatically tell me I could stick all this CISM stuff where the sun doesn't shine before he threw my ass overboard. To my surprise it was quite the opposite. He stopped chewing on his cigar, removed it from his mouth, and said quietly, "I wish you guys were around 27 years ago when I signed on." Then he shook my hand and went on his way.

The 10 days Guy and I spent at the recovery location proved to be thoroughly exhausting. We set up a 24-hour rotating shift to ensure that every boat arriving at the pier with evidence or remains would be met by a pair of CISM experts as each vessel docked. We ate when we could, and slept when we could, but it was not a sound sleep. We dealt with horrific situations as we tried to preserve U.S. Coast Guard careers while avoiding federal politics.

As sincere and important as our message was, sometimes it was difficult to see the forest for the trees. In others words, sometimes CISM team members failed to adhere to the message they were giving to others.

MY MELTDOWN

On day eight after the crash I decided I needed a little break. I needed to leave the Coast Guard station for a breath of fresh air. I walked past the five or six security checkpoints, and past a sea of media and satellite trucks, and I sought sanctuary in the peaceful  and tiny town of East Moriches, New York. While walking past an elementary school, I saw a cyclone fence with what appeared to be hundreds of purple ribbons tied on it. Also on the fence was a large poster, obviously created and signed by the students in the school. In large letters it read, "Flight 800, the prayers of East Moriches are with you," and the first zero in the number 800 was replaced with a single, unhappy face.

I saw the fence. I saw the ribbons. I saw the poster, and I lost it. All the sights, sounds, smells, and emotions of the last eight days came rushing back and I sat down on the sidewalk and cried uncontrollably for about 20 minutes.

For the previous eight days the CISM team had been a source of strength. We were a bastion of support for a group of incredible men and women who tirelessly fulfilled their horrific mission without question and who would work until they dropped. We were so focused on taking care of the U.S. Coast Guard personnel that we sometimes didn't take care of ourselves.

I'll be the first to say that once I "crashed and burned," it became incredibly therapeutic. I was instantly reenergized, refocused, and recommitted to continue our CISM mission. But my focus had changed. By now we had U.S. Coast Guard CISM assets from all over the country to take care of U.S. Coast Guard personnel on the scene. My mission shifted to take better care of my CISM teammates.

It was much more of a challenge trying to defuse mental health experts since they knew how the game was played and the rules of the road. I would usually start out with a subtle chat. But eventually they would catch on and would ask me with a twinkle in their eye, or a snide grin, "you're defusing me…aren't you?" Whereupon I would divulge my story of how I had just "crashed and burned," and that I didn't want that to happen to them.

Our ultimate goal was to set up a protocol by which all U.S. Coast Guard assets onshore, at sea, or in the air, would go through a formal CISM debriefing before being released and redeployed back to their home station.

Guy and I were on the scene for 10 days at the East Moriches, Long Island, U.S. Coast Guard Station and we saved at least three careers that we know of. Fortunately, all the Coasties we worked with realized that, in addition to being a member of the premier rescue service agency in the world, their gift was knowing that their training, camaraderie, and esprit de corps would support their future ambitions. That is why the U.S. Coast Guard's motto is *Semper paratis* (Always ready).

I'm proud to say that it is probably the best work Guy and I have ever done as a team; we had some of the most positive outcomes, and

our response to TWA Flight 800 remains the high point of my tenure as a CISM responder.

THE GIFT

This gift has a very unique history.

A critical incident stress debriefing is a highly structured process in which emergency responders are asked to participate through group discussions of what they have seen, heard, smelled, felt, and so on, during and immediately after "the event." It is important that each discussion be led by an experienced peer (me) and also that it is observed by a mental health professional (Guy). We usually concluded our group discussions with the comment that the tragedy each participant had just experienced had given each one of them a gift. The immediate verbal and nonverbal communication from each participant was always the same: "What the hell are you two guys talking about?" or "I don't get it. I have just been through the most horrific incident of my career, and you two whackos think I got a *gift* out of it!"

We would calmly reply that they all now had a homework assignment to fulfill. Their assignment was to seek out and discover "their" gift. It might take them a week, a month, or even a year. But the gift was out there. They just had to go find it.

I share this story with you simply to illustrate that the very assignment to find one's gift has merit in and of itself. Numerous people came up to me years later to thank me for challenging them to find their gift.

I typically heard: "It made me be a safer firefighter"; or "It made me look at my lifestyle from an entirely different perspective and it saved my marriage"; or "I had a substance abuse problem and it gave me the courage not to throw my life away." I could barely respond to their words, which were remarkable and truly touched me. Usually, "great job" or "well done" was all I could say.

This book is my homework assignment to you. Go find *your* gift.

One way may simply be to give your family the gift of a solid end-of-life plan.

As I mentioned early in this book, I have seen death and worked with the surviving families so many, many times. On nearly every occasion they were ill prepared and had no game plan for the rest of their lives. I am looking to you to take action on planning ahead. How ready is your family if the worst happens? How secure are the members of your family who might be left behind?

CHAPTER NINE

It's a Miracle—III

"If you are lost, climb, conserve, confess."

—U.S. NAVY FLIGHT MANUAL, RUMSFELD'S RULES

Sunday, March 31, 1991, dawned a beautiful day, sunny, clear, and warm. Spring was in the air and trees were starting to bud. It was going to be a great day. It was Easter Sunday. A fire alarm came in for a fairly routine car fire. However in the panic of the moment, the homeowner had failed to inform the 911 dispatcher of a significant detail. The car fire was inside the attached garage of a four-bedroom home.

Arriving fire companies found a fully involved car fire that had ignited the garage, and the fire was extending into the house. At that point in my fire service career I was a captain and was given the search and rescue assignment for the second floor. The homeowners could not confirm if anyone was upstairs. Two boys were unaccounted for. I started out with my partner to conduct a search of the second floor.

Heavy black smoke had banked down to the floor at the top of the stairs and we had to don our self-contained breathing apparatus (SCBA) masks. About 7–8 minutes into the search, my partner's Scott II-A SCBA had a failure and he was getting very little air. We talked about buddy breathing, but opted instead to go for the stairs.

By the time we got there, he was out of air and scrambled down the stairs to get outside to cleaner air. Engine companies operating hose lines to extinguish the fire got him safely outside.

There are two absolute rules in the fire service:

Rule number one: Never leave your partner.

Rule number two: Never violate rule number one.

However, when you are on an adrenaline rush, you think that you are immortal, and when you have not completed your mission, sometimes you make foolish decisions. (Back to stupid decisions again!) I continued the search upstairs—alone.

In another five minutes, I was in a bedroom and it got very, very hot. Visibility was zero, and suddenly I was disoriented. The smoke around me was heavy and looked like a cup of black coffee with little streams of cream in it. I felt as if I were trapped in a phone booth. I could feel the heat through my helmet and the back of my turnout gear. Rivers of sweat ran down my spine. When I crawled on the rug, it stuck to my gloves and knees like mozzarella cheese and every direction I turned seemed to be a dead end. Worst of all, I suspected that no one knew exactly where I was. My low air alarm went off telling me I had, at best, five minutes of air left. I began to panic. I thought of my wife, Andy. I thought of my daughter, Jen, and I thought "Great, now, every Easter from here on out is going to be remembered as the day Dad died in a fire!"

There is a phenomenon in fire behavior referred to as flashover. Flashover occurs when all the contents of a room get so hot that everything in the room bursts into flames simultaneously. No flames are needed as a source of ignition. Everything simply spontaneously combusts. The rug, the bed, the dresser, the wallpaper—everything ignites and the room temperature shoots up to 1800–2000 degrees.

No one, even a fully protected firefighter, could survive. I knew the room had flashover potential.

In an effort to quell my panic, I remembered a trick one of the "old guys" had taught me. If you're about to panic, close your eyes and count to ten. I thought he was nuts at the time, but at this point I would do anything. I tried it and it worked!

It gave my brain enough of a timeout so that my need to survive outweighed my growing panic. If I made all right turns going in, then making all left turns should get me out. I was able to orient myself to the front of the house by listening to the noise of the radio traffic and high-pitched diesel engines of the fire apparatus. I kept making left turns until I was in the hallway. Once in the hallway, I could faintly see light by the stairs. I opted to surf head first down the stairs. My air supply ran out as I passed through the front door into the yard. As I proceeded to the front yard, I threw up on a rhododendron bush.

With typical fire service compassion, one of my colleagues stopped by and said, "Bad chili, huh?" I just nodded. The truth is I was really scared. I knew the outcome could have been entirely different. Of course, at the time, twenty years ago, you didn't discuss such things as being so incredibly stupid that you almost died. And it literally took me another five or six years before I could even begin to talk about it. But I had been spared—again. And I felt once again that part of my being had been spared to allow me to continue to fulfill my mission of helping others.

After the fire had been extinguished and once the smoke had been removed, I went back upstairs to see how I had been "trapped." Apparently, I had crawled into a small alcove about four feet square below a dormer window. I had not realized a window was there because no light could penetrate the smoke. Since I could not see, I had simply kept going round and round in this little box.

The physical appearance of the room was striking. The high heat demarcation line was down to about six inches off the floor. Everything else in the room was black. The wallpaper had disintegrated. The plaster walls had spilt and cracked as any remaining moisture boiled out of it. There were char marks and paint blisters on all the furniture down to about a foot off the floor. When I opened a closet door, the suits and sports jackets were still smoldering.

Why the room did not flashover, I will never know. It's a miracle that I appreciate every day. By the way, the unaccounted for boys that I was searching for were playing with friends next door.

Once again I was spared and motivated further to carry on my mission to help others.

The incident did motivate me to become a scene safety officer, an assignment that became an irritating pain in the butt to my fire department colleagues. "Foot that ladder," "Pull your hood up," "Secure the utilities," and "We need a bail-out ladder to the second floor rear," all became my refrains. More importantly, I slowly initiated a new philosophy within the department that personal safety takes precedence over quick action. In other words, putting the fire out is obviously important but not at the expense of a severe injury to, or the death of, a crew member. For example, I had absolutely no problem using a half-million-dollar fire apparatus as a barricade to protect my guys operating at an accident or car fire on the highway. Such tactics are commonplace today, but back then, they were groundbreaking. The concept is simple: everyone goes home in the same condition in which they came to work.

CHAPTER TEN

Being an Entrepreneur

*"The entrepreneur always searches for change, responds
to it, and exploits it as an opportunity."*

—PETER DRUCKER

I have always been an entrepreneur. I vividly remember the first time I got paid. A tree trimmer was working around our house, and being a typical ten-year-old kid, I was asking way too many questions and generally being a nuisance. To keep me from getting underfoot, I was assigned to picking up twigs and small branches. At the end of the day, Jim gave me a silver dollar (remember those?) and I was thrilled. What a concept: do meaningful work and be paid for it. Wow! Of course, I immediately purchased a couple of packets of Nik'-l-Nips, the favored sugar water in wax bottles. You see, I hadn't yet learned the need to reinvest some of the profits back into the business.

Fast forward a couple of years to my paper route. The concept of work=money=fun had started to resonate with me. I wanted a blue Columbia bike and there was only one way to get it. I had to earn money to pay for it. So I checked with the local paper, *The Berkshire Eagle.* They had one paper route available, and I was told "But it is a mixed route." That didn't faze me in the least and I was on my way. The reason it didn't faze me is because I didn't ask the right question. A mixed paper route is one where you make deliveries to every second or third house on every third or fourth street, which is not very efficient, and you wind up with a much longer route. I didn't know that good entrepreneurs need to have a solid business plan before starting out. (A fact that I have never forgotten since.)

Sometimes being an entrepreneur is not everything it's cracked up to be.

LIFE LESSON NUMBER TWO (REVISITED):
EVERYTHING DOESN'T ALWAYS TURN OUT THE WAY YOU WANT IT TO.

In the '90s I worked for a medical testing firm that had a truly unique concept that worked pretty well. We performed OSHA-compliant physicals in a well-appointed, well-equipped, medical, trailer truck. When we were doing testing, the trailer truck would reside in the parking lot of the fire department or a company. We plugged into a power panel provided by the company and did comprehensive, OSHA, physical exams onsite. We were capable of carrying out hearing, vision, and pulmonary function testing, EKGs, chest X-rays, lab work, and physical exams right there in the truck. It was convenient, cost-effective, and in high demand.

When I joined the management team of that firm, we had discussions about the possibility of a partnership in the firm, depending on start-up funding, productivity, and performance goals. Once those productivity and performance goals had been satisfied, I raised the question of partnership and was told, "not quite yet." And the obvious follow-up question was, "Okay, when?" The response was, "We'll see."

At that point the career dissipation light started to blink in my head as it had when I knew I wasn't going to naval officer candidate school.

I needed to cut my losses, take out what equity I could from the firm, and move on. It was a fortuitous day when I suggested to my current business partner and close friend, Bob, that we should meet over lunch to explore potential opportunities in his firm. From a humble beginning came the greatest job I've ever had: consulting in the emergency service community.

I'm going to let you in on a little trade secret that consultants do not want you to know about. Consulting is often an incredibly straight-forward job. Companies hire consultants to fix their problems. They already *know*, by and large, what the problems are, and yet for some reason, they cannot fix them. They need an objective outsider, an objective consultant, to tell them what's wrong. It has been said that a consultant is someone who comes in, takes the watch off your wrist, and proceeds to tell you what time it is.

Our clients frequently tell Bob and me they are absolutely amazed at how rapidly we can identify problems and propose solutions. However, we do not feel that what we do is particularly unusual.

Remember that I was a fire chief and Bob was a paramedic, so rapidly sizing up an emergency and developing an immediate action plan was part of what we did every day in our emergency service careers. When working with a consulting client, we never spent much time walking around with a clipboard and a stopwatch, or forming a committee of 14 people to look for a solution, or getting hung up on analysis-paralysis. Instead, we were very comfortable talking with everyone from the chairman of the board to the folks on the loading dock. All of them knew what the problems were and where skeletons in the closet were. What they didn't know was how to process that information and develop an action plan. Fortunately, emergency service personnel are trained to do exactly that.

The following are some case studies:

One company I worked with was a small manufacturing firm in the Midwest that was having production problems. In the course of one day's consultation, two key issues were immediately identified. First, the sales department was making promises that the production department couldn't keep. The sales department was not happy, the production folks were not happy, and most important, most of the client's customers were not happy. The solution was not particularly imaginative, but it was practical. Key leaders in the sales department were put on the production line for two days. The solution to the problem became apparent and it took the firm a month to work things out. Through simple communication between sales and production, the sales department was now making promises that production could keep.

The second issue we identified was a little more delicate. It turned out that the chief financial officer did not have the experience, confidence, credentials, or common sense to fulfill the role. When I explained this to the president of the company, I was told, "You are correct. However, he's my brother-in-law." I replied politely but firmly that that was not my problem. My job was to identify solutions, and I suggested that his brother-in-law be assigned to special projects, research and development, or any other position that could be concocted since his inability to function as an effective CFO was hurting the company.

The role of the consultant is not to get everyone to sit in a circle, hold hands, and sing "Kumbayah." Consultants are retained to identify problems and provide solutions that are quantified and measurable. It could be as simple as putting the fire out, treating someone having a heart attack, or getting sales and production staff to actually talk to each other. Either way, it's clearly not rocket science.

On another project, we were retained by a large, national, household-brand company to evaluate a new foam product it had developed and thought might be applicable in certain firefighting applications. This foam application had come out of the research and development department as it experimented with soapy materials. We were approached to help the company develop a marketing plan to bring this firefighting foam to market.

After meeting with folks in the R&D department and marketing department, we took less than one day to recommend that they not attempt to bring this particular product to the fire service marketplace. To say there was a deer-in-the-headlights look around the conference table when we met with senior management and marketing personnel would be an understatement. Their response was quick and to the point. They said, "But we're a prestigious company known for our quality. Everyone will want this product." Our response was that they did not understand the emergency service marketplace. Their product was going to be much more expensive than the leading product in the market and their only competitor held the vast majority of the market share.

The critical point that took time for them to understand is that marketing in the emergency service marketplace is not typical. You might see ads and pictures in the glossy emergency service periodicals or run into vendors pitching their wares at national trade shows. But true marketing in emergency services takes place person to person with the guy next door.

There's an old saying: telephone, telegraph, or tell a fireman. It is one of the most instantaneous and concise communications networks in the world. And I believe it!

Whether you're looking to buy a new fire hose, new cardiac monitors, or new portable radios, you probably won't spend a lot of time doing exhaustive research on the Internet. Rather, you spend time on the phone calling your colleagues in your five neighboring towns to see what equipment they are using. The best endorsements in the world come from trusted colleagues who say that they use ABC equipment and are happy with it. Conversely, it can be the kiss of death for future sales when an emergency service colleague says that XYZ equipment is subpar and he/she would never buy it again.

The company that consulted us on its firefighting foam is a Fortune 500 company, has brands that we are all familiar and comfortable with, and has been very successful in the marketplace. What the company executives failed to grasp was the unique marketplace in which they were intending to sell their new product. They thanked us for our candor and for our concise response, and elected to follow our recommendation and not pursue marketing their fire suppression foam. Additionally, they calculated that we saved them $5,000,000 by avoiding what would have been a failed marketing effort.

Let's reflect for a moment about the difference between customers and clients. To Bob and me it is an incredibly simple concept to grasp, and yet time after time we see companies that fail to get it. Think of specific businesses you choose to patronize among several you could have chosen—for example, gas stations, drug stores, supermarkets, and so on. In those situations you are simply a customer and how hard do those firms work at keeping your business? Is it a coincidence that professionals such as doctors, lawyers, and accountants all refer to their customers as clients? No. Time and time again the businesses that want their patrons to come back all have great customer service and say a simple thank you for doing business with them. Again, it's not rocket science, it's just common sense.

In the words of Sam Walton, the founder of Wal-Mart, "There is only one boss, the customer. And he can fire everybody in the company from the chairman on down, simply by spending his money somewhere else."

Think about it: when was the last time you were so disgusted with the service you received that you told yourself you'd never go there again? More often than not it is something that is incredibly simple to fix. How about the store employee who replied to a question with "I dunno" and walked away? Or perhaps it was the waiter whose sole objective was to get you out of there as soon as possible, or the two workers at the local coffee shop who thought it was much more important to discuss the outcome of last night's episode of *American Idol* rather than wait on you. My all-time favorite negative customer service is the 1-800 telephone number that is an automated telephone tree with 12 options.

Probably the most rewarding and the most challenging achievement for entrepreneurs is to have their name on the door. If you make it, you can celebrate your just rewards. If you fail, you have no one to blame but yourself. With all that said, as an entrepreneur and business owner, I wouldn't want it any other way.

As an entrepreneur, I can give you one simple solution that I guarantee will lead you to the success of your organization.

LIFE LESSON NUMBER FOUR:
TAKE CARE OF THE TROOPS.

We allow associates in our company to see how the organization is managed. We let them know that they have a say in how the organization is run, and most important of all, at all times, we show them that we care about them. We know the names of all their children and what activities the children are involved in. (We recognize that there are periods within any company when it's time for all hands on deck, and there are periods where things can slow down a bit.) And last, we thank them and reward them for the great work that they do.

We need to set goals for productivity and profit. These goals do not necessarily carry with them a negative connotation. Goals can be created and setting them can be a creative team-building exercise. Here's what we do in our company.

We developed a program that allows us to set clear and concise company goals. It's called the annual-company-strategic-planning trip, and this is how it works. Each January we set production goals for every month of the coming year. The goals must meet the needs of the organization; they need to be understood by the team; they need to be achievable; and most important, they need to enhance customer service.

The monthly goals serve as a benchmark by which to monitor progress throughout the course of the year. In some months a goal may fall short and in other months a goal may be exceeded. The final measure comes at the end of 12 months when the net average of all the monthly goals is put together, and that number has to equal or exceed 100 percent of the goal projection developed 12 months earlier.

When the annual goal is achieved, and it usually is, we take all of our team members, including spouses, significant others, and all of their children, for a one-week, all-expense-paid, strategic-planning trip. The team members get to choose where they want to go. We have been to Disneyworld three times and gone on seven cruises over the last twelve years.

Now, you may be thinking, "Wow! That must cost a lot of money." From our perspective it doesn't 'cost' us a cent. The productivity goals are designed to reward our clients, which obviously pleases them, and we hope we've kept their repeat business as a dividend. More important, the program creates additional benefits that we didn't foresee early on, and these have turned out to be priceless.

Since our annual company strategic-planning-trip program started, we have had zero employee turnover, other than when a spouse is relocated. We have no tardiness and no abuse of sick time. We have very few human resource issues and we have an incredibly loyal team that takes care of and covers for one another when problems arise at home. It is an incredibly simple system that yields huge benefits. We are sometimes dumbfounded when other companies fail to see the merits of this team building approach.

As I think back over my business career, I realize there were some things I could have done differently. Does it matter? No. I made the best decision I could, based upon the knowledge I had at the time. But there is a common thread between firefighting and business. In both cases you need an exit strategy. In the fire service your training includes planning an alternative escape route when fighting a fire. In business you also need to design alternative exit strategies.

HAVE A BUSINESS SUCCESSION PLAN

"Thinking well is wise; planning well is wiser;
doing well is wisest and best of all."

—MALCOLM FORBES

This is a special section. It is designed to help folks who are currently owners of a business or partners in a business.

If you are not a business owner or partner, you have the option to skip this section. If you are an owner or partner, pay attention. Business succession planning is one of the most commonly over-looked aspects of managing a business.

Here are some hard questions you need to address. If you were to grab your chest and die of a heart attack today, what would happen to your business? What happens to your interest in the business? What happens to your family's interest in the business? To be less dramatic, let's say you simply want to retire from the business tomorrow and go play golf every day. What plan is in place for you to cash in your portion of the business? Will it be a lump-sum payment or will it be scheduled to be paid out over time? An exit strategy is an imperative that needs to be in place in writing, for every business and business partner.

Perhaps you don't want to fully retire but work only 2–3 days a week. How do you plan that?

Perhaps you have some patents or intellectual property that you own. Will they go with you when you leave or stay with the business?

Last but not least, let's look at some other possibilities in between. What would happen if you had a stroke and became disabled, if you embezzled $100,000 and went to jail, or you knew you'd never stop working and wanted to die at your desk?

If you can say that you and your business partner(s) already have mutually agreed-upon business succession plans to deal with each of these scenarios, and you have memorialized the agreements in writing, congratulations! Well done.

If you cannot say that, you have some more work to do.

First things first. The business owners and partners need to get together and mutually agree on what should happen when one of them leaves the company for whatever reason. You need to find a lawyer who can assist you with business succession planning. It is critical that everything be put in writing to assure that the end game has no surprises.

Professional legal help is absolutely necessary to craft accurate documents affirming who does what, who gets what, and when, if a partner departs or becomes incapacitated. The goal is to prevent disputes before they even begin. While it is not the best metaphor, you can think of a buy-sell document as a business prenuptial agreement. However, when you find a great lawyer who can walk you through the minefield of business succession planning, he/she is worth every dollar.

SO HOW DOES A BUY-SELL AGREEMENT WORK?

Of all the variations outlined above, let's deal with the simplest (but most unfortunate) outcome of the death of a partner. Most buy-sell agreements lay out a plan in which the deceased partner's interest in the business will be bought out. The surviving heirs agree to relinquish their interest or stock certificates in the business. The funding for the business buyout is usually done through a life insurance policy of which the company is the beneficiary, and it receives the cash to purchase the deceased partner's interest in the business.

Here's an example. Ted and Tom are both 50 percent owners of a trucking business that is incorporated. Ted and Tom both hold 100 shares of stock in the company. When Ted dies, the company receives the proceeds of Ted's buy-sell life insurance policy. The company (i.e., Tom) now takes that cash from the insurance payout to Ted's heirs and buys back Ted's 100 shares of stock.

Pretty simple right? True. But only if all the players (Ted, Tom, and all of their respective heirs) are up to speed on the buy-sell agreement. Can you imagine the additional trauma Ted's widow would face if Tom suddenly presents the cash to her and then demands the stock certificates back and she (1) does not know it is coming and (2) does not want to give up her rights to the business or (3) doesn't even know where the stock certificates are?

The end game of a well-designed business plan is that there are no surprises.

WHO DECIDES WHAT THE COMPANY IS WORTH?

The answer is that the partners determine the company's worth long before any succession issues may arise. Typically, the valuation of the business can take place at the annual meeting of the corporation. At that point the value of the company, or the value of one share of stock, is determined by the voting partners and recorded in the minutes of the annual meeting. Those values remain in effect until the next annual meeting. It is also recommended that the business creates a mutually agreed-upon standard formula that will be used to calculate the company's value every year. One can also use an independent auditor to evaluate and determine the value of the company. Either way, no surprises.

WHAT IS KEY MAN INSURANCE?

Key man insurance is an additional insurance policy taken out by the company on each of the partners. Should a partner die, it will take time and money to recruit and fill the vacated position. The proceeds from the key man policy help the company with recruitment costs and any additional temporary help as needed.

HOW DOES IT WORK IF A PARTNER JUST WANTS TO LEAVE?

The partners need to meet and mutually agree, as a group, on separations and buyouts. There are so many possibilities that they can't be listed here. But, you get a sense of some of the things that *could* happen on the first page of this section. Allow the lawyer to create the business succession document that fulfills the mutually agreed-upon wishes of the partners. I concede that it may not be easy for the partners to talk about all the "what ifs" in life, but it has to be done. The challenge that these discussions will entail pales in comparison to the chaos that will ensue if you don't.

WHAT IF YOU SELL THE ENTIRE BUSINESS?

The same rules apply. Remember, the buy-sell agreement is a written agreement between the partners. Whether one partner leaves the business, or all the partners decide to leave (i.e., sell) the business, there still must be written rules for who gets paid for what.

At the end of the day you really have only two choices. You can plan for all the logical ways in which a partner can leave the business and what the mutually agreed-upon rules are. Or, you can elect to do nothing and risk chaos, anarchy, and lawsuits that won't be resolved for years. Unfortunately, resolution of the conflicts could absorb all of the money that could have been shared with your family.

✓ HOT TIP ────────────────────

Plan the work, and then work the plan.

────────────────────────────

CHAPTER ELEVEN

September 11

*"Terrorist attacks can shake the foundations of our biggest buildings,
but they cannot touch the foundation of America. These acts
shatter steel, but they cannot dent the steel of American resolve."*

—GEORGE W. BUSH

It was a warm, sunny, Tuesday in September. Most of my fire department's command staff were to fly to Wisconsin to evaluate new fire apparatus we had purchased. Their plane never got off the ground.

Sometimes people wonder why they can vividly remember tragic events: whom they were with, what they were wearing, or what the weather was when the event occurred. To put things in perspective: where were you when President Kennedy was assassinated? Where were you when Bobby Kennedy and Martin Luther King were shot? And where were you during the Columbia and Challenger space shuttle disasters? Finally, where were you when you first heard about the attack on America on September 11, 2001?

The reason we have such vivid memories of those events is that our mind treats them like the critical incidents that they were. During a traumatic event, adrenaline and endorphin chemicals enter into your bloodstream and various other physiological events take place. These changes make your memory very vivid, and those tragic events are then easy to pull out of your mental-health filing cabinet.

In the case of 9/11, clearly one of the emotional triggers was the enormity of the event: a terrorist attack on America that took place simultaneously in our financial center, our military center, and very nearly, the political center of our country. The loss of life was enormous and the tragic impact even greater. Nearly 3,000 people lost their lives that day and the vast majority were simply going to work. The need for CISM of both emergency responders and civilians was overwhelming.

Another special person in my CISM family is Vic. Vic was a survivor of a Hackensack Ford fire in 1988. In that fire, five Hackensack firefighters lost their lives in the line of duty and Vic was nearly one of them. A CISM team went to Hackensack and, in Victor's words, saved his career. He too felt the calling to pay back the system, and he became another key CISM player. Vic lived in northern New Jersey and his team was immediately activated following the tragic events of 9/11. He called me and asked me to augment his team as they were being deployed to assist the Port Authority of New York and New Jersey, which managed the World Trade Center complex.

Regardless of how much experience the CISM specialists had had in their careers, nothing could have prepared them for the tragic events of 9/11. While it would be easy to become overwhelmed by both the tragedy and the mission to be accomplished, that simply was not an option. A lot of questions might be answered at a later date, but that Tuesday, we had to deploy and support the members of our police, fire, and EMS brotherhood. Was it hard? Yes. Was it emotional? Absolutely. But most important, we needed to support our emergency service brothers and sisters and families of the deceased in their greatest time of need.

Along with the World Trade Center complex, the Port Authority of New York and New Jersey is also responsible for all three major airports in the New York City area: JFK, LaGuardia, and Newark. One of my initial assignments was to work with the fire department personnel at one of the airports to simply do head checks and provide them a forum to discuss their response and to ventilate if they wanted to.

One of the key principles of CISM is peer support, which means support of one police officer by another police officer, one firefighter by another firefighter, one paramedic by another paramedic, and so on. While working at one of the airport departments, I was surprised to learn that the airport firefighters are actually sworn Port Authority police officers who also have specialized aircraft-crash, fire-rescue training.

As one can imagine, there is a long history of bantering between members of the fire service and other law enforcement agencies regarding whose job is more important, whose job is more dangerous, whose job better supports public safety, and so on. Fortunately for me, most of the folks I encountered at the airports respected me as a firefighter and allowed me to enter into some important one-on-one discussions without getting into the whole cop versus firefighter debate.

My most vivid remembrance of 9/11 has nothing to do with the loss of life, the mountains of debris, or anger at the terrorists. Maybe it was a self-defense mechanism to insulate me against all those horrific images I saw, smelled, felt, and heard. We all saw, too many times, the images of the planes hitting the towers and the towers collapsing. I have a more important memory.

That memory is of St. Paul's Chapel, which is part of Trinity Episcopal Church. The chapel was built in 1766, and George Washington worshiped there when New York City was the country's first capital. The chapel sits on the east side of the former World Trade Center site and is directly adjacent to where building five of the World Trade Center once stood. There is no good explanation for why St. Paul's Chapel was not obliterated or completely destroyed during the attack. That said, it was truly an inspiration to see the spire of St. Paul's Chapel standing tall among so much devastation and debris.

The chapel became a sanctuary for emergency response personnel. It was off-limits to everyone else. But firefighters, police officers, and construction workers could find refuge in a quiet place where unnamed volunteer heroes worked round the clock to provide food, comfort, and a blanket for workers to catch a quick nap in a pew. Over time, other volunteers came, and they included massage therapists and chiropractors and even musicians who would play soothing music.

Part of what CISM teams do is to bring control out of chaos, and as I noted during my discussion of TWA 800, the teams need to have someone take care of them as well. Those incredible resources were provided by outstanding people whose names I will never know. They provided warmth and comfort and sanctuary in the tiny chapel of St. Paul's.

When I first sought refuge in the chapel, the small cemetery out front was littered with paper and moonscape dust. People's clothing still hung in festoons from the trees surrounding the chapel, and I pondered the symbolism of the pulverized remains in the dust that could now be part of this cemetery. But once you entered the chapel, you immediately felt safe and protected. You were sheltered from the noise, the lights, the sounds, the smells, the trauma, and the media at Ground Zero. There were memorial banners hung from the chapel balcony and letters of support written by schoolchildren around the country.

Scores of books have been written about the events of 9/11 and both the heroic and horrific events that took place in and around the twin towers, at the Pentagon, and in fields of Pennsylvania. While they are all important, and they all have their own story to tell, my most important take-away from September 11, my fondest memory, is a place of safety, rest, and refuge known as St. Paul's Chapel.

Remember, nearly 3,000 innocent people went to work that day and never came home. Life is very precious and very fragile.

END-OF-LIFE PLANNING

"Always go to other people's funerals. Otherwise, they won't come to yours."

—YOGI BERRA

End-of-life planning is one of the most challenging topics to discuss and requires one to answer some very difficult questions. This section is one of the most important for your surviving family to know because they want to fulfill your wishes when you pass away.

It is understandable that you may feel a little uncomfortable thinking about the terms of your death. The good news is that you now have the luxury to plan your service exactly as you would like to have it orchestrated. You can have as little, or as much, fanfare as you desire.

Here are some basic points to explore:

- Would you like to be buried in a coffin?
- Would you like to be cremated and buried?
- Would you like to be cremated and kept in an urn?
- Would you like to be cremated and your ashes spread at a specific location?
- Would you like to have a prepurchased funeral plan?
- Has your burial plot been purchased?
- Would you like a public or private funeral?
- Whom would you like to have as pall bearers?
- Are you eligible for military honors?
- Do you have any requests for a eulogy?

Once you get through these important elements, determining the rest of the planning (scriptures, songs, reception, etc.) is somewhat easier.

As an example to assist you in working through this section, let me provide you with an overview of some of the outcomes my close friend and business partner, Bob, desires when he passes away. Bob wants to take an entirely atypical route. He wishes to be cremated. His friends and family will fly to Key West, which is one of his favorite places on the planet. His ashes will then be mixed with a bottle of Bob's favorite rum, Bacardi 8. Bob and his Bacardi 8 will then be joined with the Florida Straits out at sea just off Key West as the sun slowly sets in the west. Everyone will return to shore for a memorial celebration to be held at *Irish Kevin's Bar* on Duval Street.

Let's take a minute to discuss the disposal of loved ones at sea. The EPA even has a regulation about that too!

40 CFR 229.1 THE MARINE PROTECTION, RESEARCH AND SANCTUARY ACT (1972)

The regulation states that cremated remains can be distributed once you are three nautical miles out at sea. Note that the burial of a body at sea is a little trickier because while you need to be three miles out you also have to be in 600–1800 feet of water based on the geographic location.

Note: You are required to notify the EPA of your actions within 30 days after the burial at sea.

FOR SOMETHING DIFFERENT

Now, an ecological alternative is for the deceased to become part of a living reef at sea. See www.eternalreefs.com for more information. With this plan, one's cremated remains are mixed with cement and molded into a hollow sphere with openings and lowered into the ocean. Thus you become part of an artificial reef. This could be your living legacy in the sea.

For more information you may want to check out the following links:

http://www.seaservices.com/index.html

http://www.seaburial.com/_Home.html

http://www.alcor.org/

http://outthere.whatitcosts.com/cryogen-frozen.htm

Last but not least, for folks who really want to be unique, you can now be "buried" in space. Well, part of you can, anyway. Your remains need to be cremated and as much of your remains as can fit into a cylinder about the size of a lipstick container can be launched into space.

See www.memorialspaceflights.com and www.spaceservicesinc.com for more details.

Some notable folks who have taken advantage of this opportunity include actor James Doohan, who was Scotty on the *Star Trek* TV show, and astronaut Gordon Cooper.

It's your call. So make it! Do it exactly as you want it.

CHAPTER TWELVE

It's a Miracle—IV

"Courage is being scared to death—and saddling up anyway."

—JOHN WAYNE

It was April and it was very unusual to have a snowstorm at that time of year. But about eight inches of heavy wet snow had fallen and it was still snowing. It weighed heavily on all the tree branches and the branches hung low in a desperate struggle to carry the burden of the new fallen snow.

The fire dispatch came in as a structure fire, and I knew we had a tough fire in the middle of a snowstorm. I arrived on the scene with the first units and began my size-up, and I was startled by what I saw. The house was a typical two-bedroom, ranch-style home. Flames were blowing out from the eaves on both ends, and a roaring conflagration could be seen through the large, living-room picture window that had yet to shatter. At this point, the number of occupants of the house and their location were unknown.

My immediate reaction was that this was probably an arson fire. My rationale for that decision was that it was unusual to have that much fire burning so soon after our dispatch and arrival. Something was not right, and it took me a while to figure out what it was.

Based on the extent of the fire on my arrival, I decided we would take a defensive position in our fire attack plan. That meant that we would not assign a crew to climb to the roof to open a ventilation hole. The integrity of the roof was in doubt. Nor would we be conducting an aggressive interior attack to extinguish the fire. In terms of fire service jargon this was a "surround-and-drown" job. A search-and-rescue effort was not an option; the situation inside the home was not survivable by any occupants. As additional apparatus arrived, we immediately set up large-diameter-hose deck guns and several 2 ½-inch hose lines, and we started applying water to the fire. We were using a minimum of 4,000 gallons of water a minute, and nothing was happening. The flames didn't darken down; there was no conversion of the black smoke to white steam. Something definitely wasn't right.

About 10 minutes into the suppression operation, one of my captains approached me and said, "We got another one, chief!" to which I replied, "Another what?" "Another structure fire right next door!" was his response. I glanced at the house on my right, about 100 feet away, and I saw heavy black smoke pushing from under the attic rafters. I called for a second alarm and began to redeploy the search-and-rescue and fire-suppression resources that I had immediately available.

A short time later, another firefighter approached me and asked if he and his engine company should tackle the other house. I pointed to the right and said, "No. I think we have it under control." He pointed to the left and said, "No. That house!" I scanned the house to my left, and saw smoke pushing out from the windows and doors. There was a dull orange glow in the bedroom windows. As luck would have it, the second-alarm fire companies were just arriving, so I assigned them directly to conduct search-and-rescue operations and establish fire-suppression efforts on what was now the third of my working structure fires, all within 500 feet of each other.

My immediate reaction was, "what the (explicative) is going on here?" Again, my initial thought was that we had an arsonist running from house to house, and the possibility of such arrogance really angered me. But as all good incident commanders need to do from time to time, I took a step back to get the big-picture view and not just deal with what seemed obvious.

What was the common denominator for these three houses? A quick survey confirmed for me that all three houses were served by the same electrical distribution transformer on a telephone pole. A heavily snow-laden branch had fallen on the primary service wires above the transformer and shorted out on the neutral leg of the electrical power service lines going to all three houses. Stated differently, the circuit breaker panels in each house were now energized with 13,400 volts of electricity. And that meant that every outlet, every light switch, every appliance, and every cold-water plumbing fixture (cold-water plumbing fixtures are used to ground electrical service in a home) became a potential source of ignition.

Firefighters standing near the telephone pole with the damaged transformer all said they felt tingling on their feet through their rubber boots but never gave it a thought. They were concentrating on the mission at hand. The pump operators running the pumps on the fire trucks thought they might have felt tingling through their gloves, but they could not really be sure because they also felt the vibrations of the fire engine pump while it was operating. It is an absolute miracle that no firemen were electrocuted that day. I cannot explain why it did not happen because all the ingredients were present for death in the line of duty. Some things you just have to chalk up to fate.

Our standard dispatch protocol in cases of structure fires is to ask the power company to secure the utilities at the scene of the fire. On this particular morning the power company was overwhelmed with problems relating to downed wires and could not immediately report to the scene. Once we had determined the source of ignition and the acute nature of the problem, we asked the power company to expedite a lineman to the scene. The company promptly responded, the power was secured, and the fires went out almost immediately. One house was a total loss and the two others sustained significant damage. But no one died that day!

CHAPTER THIRTEEN

The Petit Fire

"Words have no power to impress the mind without the exquisite horror of their reality."

—Edgar Allan Poe

On this day, being a fireman stopped being fun. The pure joy that started at the Pittsfield Fire Department on a school trip in 1956, the benefit of serving the community, the impact of positive outcomes, the compassion of incredibly special people, the camaraderie of "the guys," and the unique pride that comes with being a firefighter was now gone.

I have often asked retired fire service friends, "How will you know when it's time to retire?" The answer is always the same: "You'll just know!" After the Petit fire, I knew too.

The day was July 23, 2007. And on that morning one of the most horrific assault, kidnapping, rape, murder, and arson cases in U.S. history took place in my town. On that morning, two men looking for cash and valuables broke into a house, and the crime escalated horribly. The end result was that the father was severely beaten and nearly killed with a baseball bat, the mother was raped and strangled to death, and two daughters aged 11 and 17 were tied to their beds and sexually assaulted.

Out of fear that DNA evidence might be traced to them, the men decided to pour gasoline over the dead mother, and around the two girls still alive upstairs. Additional gasoline was strategically poured throughout the house, which was set ablaze as the men left it. The father escaped through a basement hatchway only moments before the entire house erupted in flames.

Through the prudent actions of law enforcement officers I know well, the men were apprehended before they could leave the devastating scene. The fire department responded to a fully involved structure fire and had to suffer the consequences of working to extinguish a fire at a horrific scene and, at the same time, preserve the evidence of the crime. The mother was burned severely, and the girls succumbed to their injuries and smoke inhalation. One was still tied to her bed. That day my quaint New England town lost its innocence.

Three years later, the convicts were sent to death row in Connecticut, but whether they will actually be executed remains in question since Connecticut outlawed the death penalty after their conviction. I, for one, am in favor of the death penalty, considering the nature of their crime. But nothing can eliminate the mental anguish and horror my fire department colleagues went through that terrible day. I tried to provide preliminary CISM support, not as a CISM responder but as a fire department colleague, but within hours, I knew I needed to step back from my CISM support role and turn that duty over to my CISM team. I was a victim too.

I knew that day that my career as an active firefighter was going to come to a close sooner rather than later.

Chapter Fourteen

The Event That Changed My Life

"If you are going to ask yourself life-changing questions, be sure to do something with the answers."

—Bo Bennett

The year was 2009 and it was time for Tim to slip back to being stupid again.

It was March 7 and St. Patrick's Day was coming. Like many New Englanders, I had spent the previous day cutting trees and splitting logs into firewood to get ready for the next winter. An old adage claims that he who heats with wood is twice warmed. You can be pretty exerted by cutting trees and splitting firewood, but I was outdoors, enjoying myself, and performing a necessary function.

I went to bed that evening with a pain in my shoulder that was obviously due to overexertion and the stress and strain of working outside. I took a couple of Advil™ tablets and went back to bed; no pain, no foul. Well, that's not entirely accurate because when I woke up the next morning after a restless night, the pain in my shoulder was still there and now moving across my left chest. I knew it wasn't anything significant but thought that perhaps the prudent thing to do was go to the hospital and get checked out. My beautiful wife went with me, and since it wasn't a big deal, I insisted on driving.

We arrived at the emergency room and I provided a brief description of my symptoms to the triage nurse, who instantly fast-tracked me through the admission process and got me a bed in room four in the emergency room. Vital signs were taken along with a history and physical. I was hooked up to a cardiac monitor and more tubes of blood were taken than I could count. Then there was peace and harmony for about 20 minutes.

Suddenly, the curtain was thrown back and three physicians, four nurses, three physicians' assistants, and, I think, a janitor descended upon me. Clothes were cut off and IVs were started in both arms, and nitroglycerin was placed beneath my tongue. All of this seemed to take place in a matter of seconds before I was able to say, "Excuse me. I'm the patient here. What is going on?" A physician, whom I got to know very well, informed me that I had had a minor heart attack.

The word *minor* resonated with me. Is having a minor heart attack like being a little bit pregnant or saying that we're only going to amputate a minor part of your leg? In my book there was no such thing as a *minor* heart attack.

The crowd of medical professionals started to thin out once I was stabilized. I told one of the nurses that I still needed to know what was going on. She said, "Your lab test results came back and your CKMB is elevated. It looks like you are a good possibility for angio, but I'm not sure if they will use a full metal jacket or not." Then she gave me a blasé look, turned, and walked away.

She fell into an old trap that is easy for any of us to do. Sometimes we get very comfortable with the acronyms and vocabulary of our respective organizations and forget that the customer or client has no clue what we are talking about. It's like that old classic line from the Paul Newman film *Cool Hand Luke,* "What we've got here is [a] failure to communicate."

As a guy who has spent years working in a level 1 trauma center, I knew exactly what she meant, and yet, as a patient, I freaked. Imagine if I had no clue what she was talking about!

Here is the translation. There are two cardiac lab tests called creatinine kinase MB (CKMB) and the troponin test. They measure isoenzymes in the blood that are released when the heart becomes severely stressed. An elevated value may indicate a heart attack within the last eight hours. If the heart attack is caused by a blockage of the heart vessels, a balloon angioplasty procedure may be necessary. During a balloon angioplasty, the doctor threads a thin tube through a blood vessel in the groin up to the blockage in the artery of your heart. The tube has a tiny balloon on the end. When the tube is in place, the doctor inflates the balloon to push the blockage material, called plaque, outward against the wall of the artery. This widens the artery and restores blood flow. It's analogous to a miniature snow plow.

To keep the vessel walls from recollapsing, a medical stent is left in place. Think of it as a small pipe left in your heart. There are different kinds of stents. Most are made of a metal, or plastic, mesh-like material. A drug-eluting stent is coated with an anticoagulant medicine that further helps prevent the arteries from reclosing. The artery stent is left permanently in the heart. I had the pleasure of getting two stents placed in my heart.

When I consulted my doctor, he said that I had an 85 percent blockage in my left anterior descending artery and that the situation could be repaired using angioplasty. Having been a fire service instructor for years and knowing the value of paraphrasing a process in the simplest of terms, I paraphrased it this way: "So Doc, let me get this straight. You're going to cut into a vein in my groin, thread a small balloon through my blood vessels to my heart, blow up the balloon to open the artery, back the balloon out, and go in again and push a medical stent into my left anterior descending artery and leave it there?"

His response was pretty simple. He said, "Pretty much." The fact that my heart attack was "minor" meant that I did not need to immediately be rushed into the cardiac catheterization operating room to be operated on. I was allowed to stabilize with additional medications overnight.

While I will never be able to prove it, I highly suspect that the ER triage nurse wrote in big black letters on my medical chart, "This is the stupid fireman who drove himself to the hospital" because every physician, physician's assistant, nurse, and technician who came into my room said, "Oh, you're the one!" Subtext: *How could a knowledgeable firefighter be so stupid to think that driving himself to the hospital was a good idea when he had the signs and symptoms of a heart attack?*

As I was being prepped for the procedure—my groin needed to be shaved—I asked the nurse if she might be kind enough to leave a small shamrock for my wife? It was St. Patrick's Day. She replied, "You're the firemen, aren't you?" "Yes," I replied proudly. And then I was lambasted again for driving myself to the hospital. Man, this was a tough crowd.

In the end, the procedure went very well, and my life was dramatically changed. Having a heart attack is a game changer. Before the attack, if you had told me that I could get by with one small coffee with a little skim milk in it per day, I would've called you crazy. But my lifestyle is forever changed: my diet has changed, my respect for exertion has changed, and my beautiful bride has become a loving and caring command master chief when it comes to food. As much as she may be overreaching with her food restrictions and label reading, I love her dearly for making me walk the straight and narrow. "Everything in moderation" is now my new mantra.

Note: My heart attack was due in part to stressors on the job. When an alarm comes in at night, a firefighter's body takes a toll, going from a sound sleep to turbo-charged in three seconds. Again, the repeated chemical dump of adrenaline and endorphins has a negative impact on our cardiac system. And that is why heart attacks continue to be a major cause of death in the fire service. Moderation in food, alcohol, cholesterol intake, smoking, and so on, will help to reduce stress on your heart. Starting today, take charge and be more aware of how much you eat, drink, and smoke.

✓ HOT TIP ───────────────

What does the number 3,311,280,000 represent?

───────────────────────────

Is it the number of dollars wasted every four years on political campaign advertising? No.

Is it the number of light years to the outer reaches of our galaxy? No.

Is it the number of barrels of oil yet to be pumped out of the earth? No.

It is the number of heartbeats that healthy people will have from the day they are born until the day they die at the age of ninety. It is a finite number produced by an electromechanical pump. Each beat of your heart is priceless. It is one cycle that you can never get back. Heartbeats are like time. As each second passes, it is gone, and gone forever. The question is how many heart beats have you wasted away and by how many days, weeks, or years will you die prematurely because of it?

Let's do some math: You are born and it's a great day. A normal heart beats around 70 beats per minute. Doing the math: 70 beats per minute times 60 minutes in an hour times 24 hours in a day times 365 days in a year times 90 years equals 3,311,280,000.

Each heart beat pumps about 2–3 ounces of blood through the body. That translates to 1.5 gallons a minute, 2,160 gallons a day, 788,400 gallons a year, and 71 million gallons over the years to age ninety.

Now what other mechanical pump can do nearly as well? None! The fuel pump in your car can do up to about half a gallon a minute and how long do fuel pumps last? A revved-up fire engine can do 1,500 gallons a minute but only for a short duration of time. There is no pump that is as efficient and long lasting as the human heart. But even our hearts have a finite life span and will eventually wear out.

Let's examine for a minute how you may be "wasting" heart beats and therefore lowering the number of heart beats you have left and shortening your life span.

STRESS

There is no doubt that high anxiety or having chronic high levels of stress takes a toll on your heart. Let's say you're driving to work and you have a road rage incident. You get angry, share a single digit wave with the other driver, saying, "You're number one with me," and compete with the other driver for the rest of your commute to work. What was the outcome and how many heartbeats did you waste? Sometimes your kids can really drive you nuts, and you begin raising your voice at them, and your blood pressure goes up. It could be that you feel they waste too much time watching DVDs, they fail to do their part of household chores, or they want to leave the house looking like slobs. And you go crazy. A lot of our behavior needs to be modified. Ask yourself how many heartbeats you will waste until you stop getting overexcited.

Examples of extremely stressful situations include the death of a family member, going through a divorce, and holidays—yes, holidays.

There is no doubt that the death of a family member carries with it a great deal of pain, grief, and stress. Some stress can be reduced by discussing and preplanning with your loved ones what they would like to have happen when they die. Want to learn more? Check out and download a free copy of my report *Terminal Programming* from my website. Go to www.timpelton.com/terminalprogram- ming. Funerals are never easy, but some advanced funeral planning will clearly reduce the stress levels a bit and save a few of those very valuable heartbeats.

Here is another take-away for you. Making funeral arrange- ments at the funeral home is highly emotional and traumatic. It's easy to get caught up in the jargon of the funeral director. You may not understand it all or the situation may be too emotional for you to ask questions. You should consider doing some homework now, when there is no pressure. What are the laws in your state? What is the price difference between cremation and a casket burial? What are the benefits available for veterans? Ask now, not later.

It is very rare that a divorce is not a stressful event. Issues are often clouded by pride, ego, tenacity, control, money, children, pos- sessions, and who "wins." As common as they are, all divorces are unique. In the event you are going through a divorce or have been through one already, I ask you what the outcome was and how many heartbeats you wasted?

Folks are often surprised when I comment that holidays can be a stressful time. But think about it for a second. At Christmas or Hanukah people often spend hours and even days searching for the perfect gift. Just circling the parking lot in the mall looking for a parking place can take an hour. And let's not forget the command-performance, family, "we-have-to-go" road trip(s) to see both sets of grandparents, requiring the movement of more material than was used in the D-Day landing in Normandy. That stress is only compounded when there is just one guy working at the toll booth on the interstate on Christmas Day. And, in addition, you are reminded, "I *told* you we should have gotten one of those E-Z Pass toll things!" Are we having fun yet?

Think about Thanksgiving. You and your significant other plan the purchase of food a week in advance and feverishly cook for 24–36 hours beforehand. The food is served at a beautifully set table with a new linen table cloth and new candlesticks, and the only thing Uncle Louie has to say is, "What! No cranberry sauce?" The herd consumes copious amounts of food at the table and retires to the living room to fall asleep watching football. This, of course, is immediately followed by the exhausted host and hostess collapsing in the corner, and they haven't even cleaned up yet!

Make a commitment to yourself that it is okay to say no. It is okay to say no to your mother-in-law who has lobbied you with, "So you're doing Thanksgiving again this year, right, dearie?" It is okay to say no when you are invited to yet another command-performance gathering of the family at Christmas. I have been there and done that and learned to save countless heartbeats that would otherwise have been wasted.

SMOKING

There are volumes of data on how harmful smoking is to the heart, and it is not my plan to discuss them here. Smoking is a personal choice, and you, and only you, define your reason for smoking. That said, I would be remiss if I did not challenge you with a few questions.

Why did you start smoking? A lot of people started smoking as teenagers to "fit in with the big kids" and feel like a grown-up. Well, you're 47 years old now, and I think we can all agree that the original goal has been met.

"Smoking helps me relax." Scores of people I have spoken to have shared that comment. I suggest, however, that there are several alternatives to help you relax in lieu of smoking, none of which weaken your heart or cause lung cancer.

"Smoking tastes good." Now here is where I need some help. As a former smoker who quit over 40 years ago, I suspect the taste of cigarettes has not evolved dramatically over that period. The taste, I recall, is somewhere between licking the inside of the muffler on your car and running your tongue along the chalk tray beneath the blackboard in high school. There are not many things that I am adamant about, but trying to convince me that taste is a valid reason to smoke will never fly.

I suggest that smoking has an enormous impact on wasting heartbeats, and if you don't die from cardiac failure, lung cancer will probably kill you.

Think about it, what is the risk/benefit ratio of smoking with regard to cost and health?

So how do you quit? You quit in your head. You and you alone need to convince yourself that a long life has a greater reward than all the "pleasure" that smoking allegedly gives you. Do you want to see your kids get married? You have worked incredibly hard all you life and wouldn't it be great to retire and enjoy life for the next 20+ years? Go ahead and enjoy your pension plan, you worked hard for it and deserve to get the most out of it.

It's your call. You need to make it! Nicotine patches may help, or hypnosis may get you started, but the only way you can truly quit smoking is to appreciate that the benefits far outweigh the risks.

DIET

My goal here is not to promote the Atkin's Diet, the South Beach Diet, low carbs, no carbs, and so on. I simply want to share a concept and thought process with you. It stands to reason that if I had you put on a backpack with 25 pounds of rocks in it and had you walk up five flights of stairs, your heart would be pumping a little harder. Now, lose the visual image of the backpack but ask yourself the question, "Am I carrying 25 or more extra pounds around than I should?" If you answered yes, I encourage you to think about how many heartbeats you are wasting *every day* as you walk around, go shopping, or take care of the kids?

The goal is very simple. I want you to appreciate that the human heart is an electromechanical device, a very efficient one, but still an electromechanical device. It has just so many heart beats in it. What you can do, starting today, is minimize the number of heart beats you waste and can never get back! Apply some common sense, a little behavior modification, some moderate life-style changes, and you will dramatically increase your longevity and quality of life.

Just why do I think this information is important? It's simple. I survived a heart attack.

Having a heart attack is a pretty harsh reality check. You either learn from it and move forward, or you don't, and you die. I was clearly shocked about what happened and assigned it to the lessons-learned category. This life-changing event became one of the major motivations for writing *The Ultimate Family Gift.*

It also motivated me to develop an estate plan.

DEVELOPING AN ESTATE PLAN

"Methods of escape or intended escape from tax liability are many. Some are instances of avoidance, which appear to have the color of legality; others are on the borderline of legality; others are plainly contrary even to the letter of the law."

—FRANKLIN D. ROOSEVELT

The goal of this section is to tie together all the information you have received up to this point. By now you should be thinking in terms of finding a lawyer, accountant, insurance agent, and banker to help you with your planning efforts. Now you have just added a financial planner to your team.

To use a football analogy, you are the head coach. The game is to strategically plan the rest of your life, including the "overtime period" after you die. You have an offensive coordinator, also known as a lawyer. You have a defensive coordinator who is your accountant. Your insurance agent is your special team coach, and the banker is your recruiting agent. They will provide incredible insight for you and will help you plan for the rest of your life.

THE FOLLOWING ITEMS SHOULD BE CONSIDERED PART OF ONE'S ESTATE PLAN:

- real estate
- personal property (cars, boats, jewelry, etc.)
- bank accounts
- retirement plans (pensions, 401(k)s, etc.)
- stock portfolio
- life insurance proceeds (e.g., cash value of whole-life policies or the value at death of aggregate policies)
- business partnerships
- intellectual property

WHAT IS ESTATE PLANNING?

An estate plan is your effort to define and resolve any and all legal questions that may occur when you die, as well as clearly stating exactly how you want your assets distributed upon your death. The strategic part is that you want to complete your estate plan long before you pass away. The tricky part is getting together with your "teammates" to work out all the legal, probate, funding, and tax issues.

✓ HOT TIP —————————————

Your coaches may not all agree on a specific course of action, and you may need to arbitrate a workable solution. The end game is to determine what is right for you, not for them.

ESTATE PLANNING SOUNDS A LOT LIKE PLANNING A WILL. WHAT IS THE DIFFERENCE?

Your estate plan clearly articulates exactly what, and how, your assets should be distributed, as well as how any tax considerations should be managed. Your will is a broader document that covers everything else. A will is part of the planning process and estate planning will also focus on the financial, tax, medical, and business implications not outlined in one's will. It is important to do both a will and estate planning.

 **HOT TIP**

A revocable trust lets you control your assets as long as you are alive and you can identify another person to manage your affairs and assets should you become incapacitated.

IT SOUNDS AS IF ONLY WEALTHY PEOPLE NEED AN ESTATE PLAN. IS THAT TRUE?

No! Whether your estate is large or small, you still need to designate someone to manage all of your affairs when you are unable to, whether after your death or after you have become incapacitated. If you have a large estate, it is foolhardy not to have an estate plan. As an example, there are several legal methods to preserve, or postpone, the payment of estate taxes that you might otherwise give to the government instead of your heirs.

THE REVOCABLE LIVING TRUST

A revocable living trust is another tool in the estate planning play book. It is a document that allows you to place certain assets in a trust that allows you to control your assets while you are still alive. Those assets will pass directly to your beneficiaries upon your death. Most important, those assets do not pass through the probate court.

Typically, in a trust agreement, you name yourself as the trustee, managing the trust while you are alive. You also name a successor trustee to fulfill your desires and manage the trust after you die. The successor trustee acts in a similar fashion to the executor you assign in your will. However, they do not need to be the same person. You make the call.

Estate planning is not a quick process. The challenge is that all the players on your team (the lawyer, the banker, the planner, etc.) all need to agree that (1) the piece of the puzzle that they bring to the table works, but more importantly, (2) all the pieces of the estate planning puzzle will fit and work properly together. The time, effort, and expense of working through the estate planning process is well worth the effort. And remember, all this effort is not about you. It is all about taking care of your surviving family.

Cost of paper needed: $50. Cost of analysis and document preparation: $1,000. Confidence that when you die, your wishes will be fulfilled by the people you trust the most: priceless.

CHAPTER FIFTEEN

Honoring the Dead

"It is rather for us to be here dedicated to the great task remaining before us—that from these honored dead we take increased devotion to that cause for which they gave the last full measure of devotion."

—ABRAHAM LINCOLN AT GETTYSBURG

After my heart attack, I knew that my fire service career would be coming to an end. It was a young man's game and in the infamous words of Clint Eastwood, "A man's got to know his limitations." I now knew mine.

Once they've been in the fire service for a long time, most people find it very difficult to simply give up cold turkey and walk away. It's been such a special part of their life, the ups and downs, and the good times, and the bad, and all the friends and colleagues they have met are clearly special.

And thus began a new phase of my association with those who died. Having completed a fascinating, enlightening, and rewarding journey in the fire service, the question became what to do with an old fire chief nearing the end of his career, who has an incredible passion for taking care of others and for honoring those who have come before him. What do you do with a guy whose core values revolve around integrity, honor, dignity, and respect? What do you do with someone who believes that if you're on time, you're already late, has a passion to be perfect, and is looking to exchange the best job in the world for the best duty in the world?

For me, the answer was really quite simple. I became ingrained in the fire service honor guard movement at every level I could.

As you read *The Ultimate Family Gift*, I hope you grasped the concept that we really do not know when we are going to die and that preparing for that fateful day, or at least thinking about it, is critically important. My goal as you read on is for you to realize and appreciate that preparing for when you pass away is good, but taking care of the folks you leave behind is critical.

My "new" passion to help others by joining the fire service honor guards was not like taking up a new business career. Let me take a moment to explain what drove me to dedicate my life to this cause. In a previous chapter I talked about the "brotherhood" of emergency service personnel and the great pride they take in their occupations. We all recognize and appreciate the risks that come with these occupations.

Is it a coincidence that when you go to the deli, the mall, or a ballgame, you see firemen, police officers, and EMS personnel proudly wearing a T-shirt or jacket displaying the logo of their service or organization? I do not think so. The pride in the "brotherhood" is without limit. The ABC *Evening News* reported recently that over 80 percent of firefighters feel that they have the greatest job in the world.

When a fire department suffers a line-of-duty death of one of their own, it is horribly devastating. I have already shared with you several fatalities of my "brothers" within my fire department. We could not prevent their deaths, but we could still honor their service by bestowing high honors for them at their funeral. While it is a very nice statement to make, fulfilling that goal has significant challenges.

Based upon the current funeral planning protocol of my honor guard organization, hundreds of questions need to be answered by the surviving family or impacted department in the first 24 to 36 hours after someone dies in the line of duty. It takes compassion, tact, and tenacity to pull off the planning successfully. When you are dealing with multiple line-of-duty deaths, the planning needs to increase exponentially. Simply stated, the primary objective of any honor guard planning unit is to establish control in an otherwise chaotic situation. The support that the honor guard provides the fire service department helps restore the department to its operational level while recognizing that the department will be operating at a new normal. Being organized is of paramount importance. Being caring and compassionate expedites the healing process.

THE CONNECTICUT STATEWIDE HONOR GUARD (CTHG)

As this book goes to press I am currently the commander of the Connecticut Statewide Honor Guard (www.cthg.org). Our membership is entirely voluntary, and it is comprised of both career and volunteer firefighters in Connecticut who have the passion and pride to do whatever it takes to assist our brother and sister firefighters in their greatest time of need—that is, when one of their own has had an unanticipated death.

A common thread weaves throughout the entire emergency service community and that is the need for training, standard operating procedures and protocols, and discipline within the organization. However, often lacking in that education is how to conduct a high-honors funeral. Everyone knows that folding a flag is important, but exactly how should it be done? What can the department do at the wake to show its respect? What exactly is the protocol for how the casket should move? How should seating inside the church be organized? These and a host of other questions all need to be answered in a short amount of time.

The primary objective of any honor guard planning unit is to bring control out of chaos, and we approach that mission in several different ways. Our first planning guideline is to inquire if the fire department leadership has had an opportunity to meet with the surviving family and explore exactly what the family would like to have happen at the wake and funeral. The CTHG protocol calls for the surviving family, not the fire department, to drive what will happen. Adhering to that protocol sometimes creates differences of opinion that need to be tactfully worked through with solutions that are mediated between the family and the fire department.

The next planning element is to determine with the fire department leadership the exact level of participation the department would like the CTHG to fulfill. The range of services offered includes planning, training, and coaching, or having the CTHG carry out all the funeral/burial arrangements requested by the department. The CTHG prefers to take an active training and coaching role, but let the fire department itself participate in and actively manage events during the wake and funeral. However, depending upon the nature of the firefighter's death, that is sometimes not possible.

To put this in perspective, the passing of a retired fire chief may involve planning a wake and funeral service for 50 members of the department and coordinating a few hundred civilian participants. On the other hand, a line-of-duty death may entail managing 5000+ participants.

In 2010 the CTHG, in tandem with several other fire service agencies, planned for, and managed, the funerals of two Bridgeport,

Connecticut, firefighters killed in the line of duty. Both funerals were held on the same day, and the logistics included staging, organizing, and moving 10,000 emergency service personnel. The biggest challenge in planning for any emergency service funeral is that there are no "do overs." You have to get it right the first time, every time.

While a funeral for an emergency service colleague killed in the line of duty has more moving parts than a routine funeral, the basics are the same.

- Unity of command: There should be only one boss and that person needs to have the tact and skill to know exactly when to be a mentor, a mother, or a master sergeant. I call it leading from the front.

- Span of control: There is absolutely no way that chief planners have the time or energy to do it all by themselves. If they do, the event is doomed to failure immediately. Chief planners should be directly responsible for no more than one or two major planning elements. Most of their time should be spent delegating responsibility and monitoring the success (or failure) of the planning team. The solution is to pick good people. Chief planners need to know the strengths and weaknesses of the team so that they can delegate responsibility and authority accordingly. And with a little loss of objectivity, I am proud to say that the CTHG has the greatest team imaginable. There are a dozen or so go-to people, augmented by an additional 30 honor guard professionals who can clearly fulfill the need. Such a skill becomes critically important when there is a lot of planning to be done and not a lot of time to do it.

- Accountability: This is probably the most challenging element for the chief planner who has historically been an action-oriented, hands-on leader. Forming the right team and delegating authority and responsibility appropriately to independent decision makers throughout the planning process increases the likelihood that the event will be successfully executed, perhaps not the way you would have done it, but a successful completion of the mission is the ultimate goal, and that is okay.

In the words of General George Patton, "Don't tell people how to do things; tell them what needs to be done and let them surprise you with their results."

THE NATIONAL HONOR GUARD ACADEMY (NHGA)

You may be asking yourself where one goes to learn all about the proper protocols for conducting an emergency service funeral. The answer is to spend a week at the National Honor Guard Academy (www.nationalhonorguardacademy.com) on one of the courses the academy offers around the country. It is probably like no other course you've ever taken. It's a boot-camp-style course that packs two weeks of curriculum into five and a half days, and each day is 12 hours long.

The students must be highly motivated, highly focused, and willing to work hard. The days start at 6 a.m. with physical training to get the blood flowing, and they conclude at 6 p.m. with a flag retrieval and a flag folding detail. Training includes instruction on the history and traditions of emergency service funerals, marching in formation, a practice casket vigil in a funeral home, more marching, hands-on casket movements in a church, more marching, forming a color team, more marching, hands-on casket movements in the cemetery, and finally a little more marching. The outcome is that each student has an incredible set of tools to plan, organize, direct, and control a funeral for his/her organization. Graduates of the class also become part of the NHGA network of students throughout the country who are always available to provide assistance 24 hours a day, seven days a week.

The formation of the National Honor Guard Academy has an interesting history. The academy is based in Florida and was formed by a fire chief who saw a severe training void that needed to be filled. Several of the instructors of the NHGA, myself included, had taken other honor guard, academy-type classes and found them to be lacking in several aspects, mainly tradition and precision. Having identified a problem, the chief proposed a solution by creating the curriculum that is now used by the NHGA.

The National Honor Guard Academy is the premier organization in the country for training emergency service personnel in planning and executing funeral services for fallen colleagues.

Every year in October, a special fire service event takes place in Emmetsburg, Maryland, at the National Fire Academy. It's called the National Fallen Firefighter's Foundation (NFFF) Memorial Weekend. Thousands of personnel from fire departments honor guards, pipers, drummers, and volunteers who have assembled from around the country to pay honor to fallen brothers and sisters who died in the line of duty in the prior year. It is a weekend filled with pride, honor, dignity, emotion, and devotion to those members of the fire service that made the ultimate sacrifice. It is a weekend when fire service tradition meets military precision.

More importantly we pay homage to the surviving families and let them know that their loved one will never be forgotten, and that we will be there to provide support to them for the challenging years to come. Peer support groups reach out to each of the survivor families and assure them that they are not alone. Many volunteers in the support groups are survivors themselves. The weekend is spent visiting the National Memorial Chapel and the Fallen Fire-fighter Memorial, attending a candlelight vigil, and participating in a memorial service specifically designed for the survivors' deceased loved ones.

Participating in a National Fallen Firefighters Memorial Weekend is far and away one of the most rewarding things I do. Everyone's efforts are voluntary. We do not seek, nor would we accept, compensation. We do it simply because it is the right thing to do.

THE *"IT"* FACTOR

The *"It"* factor is a term coined by a close friend. It is that unique element in the human psyche that motivates people to do the right thing simply because it is the right thing to do and not because it brings personal recognition or gratitude. *"It"* is that intangible property of those who will do whatever it takes, whenever they are asked; when the mission only needs to be explained once, and it will be done successfully every time.

What motivates hundreds of firefighters to don their class A uniforms and stand in the rain outside a church during a funeral? Respect! What motivates them to practice folding a flag 20 times until the process is perfect? Honor! What motivates them to give up personal time with their families to spend days planning a funeral with an overwhelmed fire department? Duty. What motivates people to give it their all, 24/7/365, without question or discussion? Dedication.

Now, people simply have *"It"* or they don't. *"It"* can't be bought and *"It"* can't be taught. *"It"* is earned, not given. *"It"* evolves through demonstrating pride, acknowledging traditions, displaying dignity, and granting honor. I honor and thank my close honor guard colleagues who have *"It"* and for being part of my life.

> *"The true test of a man's character is what he does when no one is watching."*
>
> **—JOHN WOODEN**

In 2012 I had the honor and privilege of being the honor guard commander for the National Fallen Firefighters Foundation Memorial Weekend. To see all the flag bearers perform flawlessly, to hear the pipe band playing the Balmoral March, to have all the marching units hit their marks, and to experience 800–1,000 arms simultaneously snap a salute while surrounding the surviving families with a sea of blue uniformed personnel is a special and sacred moment. It is all done for one reason and one reason only: to honor the fallen and to support their surviving families.

ARLINGTON NATIONAL CEMETERY

As we reflect on honoring fallen heroes, there is no more hallowed ground than Arlington National Cemetery, which honors Americans who have made the ultimate sacrifice both in peace and in war. To walk the grounds of Arlington is incredibly humbling. This is where valor rests. If you have never had an emotional response regarding death or dying before, try visiting Arlington National Cemetery. If anyone ever needs a clearer understanding that freedom is not free, or wishes to see where dignity and honor rest in solemn repose, a visit to Arlington is in order.

Arlington National Cemetery was established during the Civil War. You will see the precise serrated edge of rows and rows of tombstones on over 600 acres of beautifully kept land overlooking Washington, DC. On a typical day there will be over two dozen funerals or internments conducted at the cemetery. You will often hear the clatter of a horse-drawn caisson led by the U.S. Army Third Infantry Division, the Old Guard. Frequently the cracks of three volleys of a 21-gun salute resonate over the grounds, followed by the 24 compelling notes of Taps as it is solemnly played.

There is no better place to observe the precision of bestowing honors than to visit the Tomb of the Unknowns. Here soldiers of the Third Army Infantry Division, known as Tomb Guards, march in precision and guard the tomb, which is guarded 24 hours a day, seven days a week, and that has occurred every day since April 9, 1932. The

location of the Tomb of the Unknowns is near where Confederate General Robert E. Lee maintained some of his gardens when he lived in Virginia.

The number 21 is often used to represent the highest honor in the military. The custom stems from naval tradition, in which a warship would fire its cannons harmlessly out to sea until all ammunition was spent to show that the ship was disarmed, thereby signifying lack of hostile intent. As naval customs evolved, 21 guns came to be fired for heads of state, the number decreasing with the rank of the recipient of the honor.

The Tomb Guard marches 21 steps down the black mat beside the tomb, turns, faces east for 21 seconds, turns and faces north for 21 seconds, and then takes 21 steps down the mat and repeats the process. After the turn, the sentinel executes a sharp "shoulder-arms" movement to place the weapon on the shoulder closest to the visitors, signifying that the sentinel stands between the tomb and any possible threat. The number 21 was chosen because it symbolizes the highest military honor that can be bestowed: the 21-gun salute.

Have you ever wondered who the soldier guarding the Tomb of the Unknowns is? Have you ever watched that soldier walk back and forth and then perform the incredibly impressive changing of the guards? Those soldiers go through a very rigorous training, and they are all handpicked. Each soldier must have strong military bearing, discipline and stamina, and present an outstanding soldierly appearance. Over 80 percent of the soldiers who try out for this duty do not make it. The following are some of the requirements of what the soldiers must do to qualify for the position as a guard of the Tomb of the Unknowns.

Each soldier must be able to flawlessly perform seven different types of walk, honors, and ceremonies. They must retain vast amounts of knowledge concerning the tomb, Arlington National Cemetery, the U.S. Army and their unit. A soldier must be 5' 11" to 6' 4" tall and have a 30-inch waist. It takes eight hours for these soldiers to prep their uniforms for their next guard duty at the tomb. They must memorize a 17-page manuscript and know it verbatim.

After a soldier serves nine months at the tomb and passes a series of stringent tests, a Tomb Guard identification badge is awarded. As of 2012, only 602 Tomb Guard badges have been awarded since the badge's inception. The Tomb Guard badge is considered the second highest military badge award, surpassed only by the astronaut's badge.

The shoes of the Tomb Guards are specially made with very thick soles to keep the heat and cold from their feet. The soles are built up to make them the same height as the heel. Metal heel plates extend to the top of the shoe to make the loud click as the soldier comes to a halt. That tradition comes from when cavalry soldiers first guarded the tomb. Countless hours are spent bringing the shoes to a flawless glossy shine.

If you look closely, you will see the guard makes a special roll of his foot on the outside of the sole of his shoes as he walks. This ensures that his cover [hat] and bayonet do not bounce as he walks. The downside is that it takes an orthopedic toll.

Each guard strategically dismantles his/her U.S. Army class A uniform and then meticulously re-sews it such that there are no wrinkles or folds on it.

There are three unknown soldiers resting in the tomb. They served in World War I, World War II, and Korea. A serviceman who fought in Viet Nam was originally interred in the tomb by mistake, but as more sophisticated DNA analysis came along, his body was identified. The Viet Nam crypt remains empty.

Some people think that when Arlington National Cemetery closes for the evening, "the walk" stops. Not so. The formality and precision continues uninterrupted all night. For these men and women, the nonstop walk and guard of their post is key to the honor and respect shown to the tomb's dead warriors and is symbolic of all American combat dead who are unaccounted for. The steady step in rain, sleet, snow, hail, wind, heat, and cold must be uninterrupted, which is a critical element of the honor shown.

In 2003 hurricane Isabel decimated Washington, DC. Thousands of trees were blown down. There were major power outages, and widespread flooding occurred. The commander of the U.S. Third Infantry sent word to the nighttime sentry detail to secure operations and seek shelter for their personal safety.

We all know that a soldier in the Tomb Guard would *never* disobey an order. However, in the military, as in the fire service, a little discretion is always allowed by the operational commander on the scene. One guard is alleged to have said, "No way, sir! I've got buddies getting shot at in Iraq who would kick my butt if word got out that we let them down. I have no intention of spending my army career being known as the idiot who couldn't stand a little breeze and shirked his duty."

Americans take much pride in what their military personnel do to protect their country, freedom, and rights. The Tomb of the Unknowns is a constant reminder of that pride and the honor given to soldiers who risk their lives for their country.

THE FINAL INSPECTION

It's the marine, sailor, soldier, coast guardsmen,
and airmen, not the reporter,

Who has given us the freedom of the press.

It's the marine, sailor, soldier, coast guardsmen,
and airmen, not the poet,

Who has given us the freedom of speech.

It's the marine, sailor, soldier, coast guardsmen,
and airmen, not the politicians,

Who ensure our right to life, liberty, and the pursuit of happiness.

It's the marine, sailor, soldier, coast guardsmen,
and airmen who salute the flag,

Who serve beneath the flag,

And whose coffin is draped by the flag.

In 2008 members of the CTHG and National Honor Guard Academy started the tradition of a National Fallen Firefighter's Foundation Memorial Weekend by placing a wreath in honor and memory of all of their fallen comrades at the Tomb of the Unknowns. There is no higher honor I will ever experience than that day when I placed

the wreath at the tomb in 2008. The entire ceremony only took a few minutes. But, to stand briefly on that hallowed space and to place a memorial wreath there on that beautiful fall day, while looking down upon the Lincoln Memorial, Washington Monument, and U.S. Capitol building as Taps played respectfully in the background was a moment like no other. The honor and pride one feels is beyond measure, and even talking about it now, years later, makes me pause, take a deep breath, and compose myself.

Years later another special event occurred at the Tomb of the Unknowns. It was Thursday, October 12, 2012. It was my year to be the commander of all the honor guard elements of the NFFF

Memorial Weekend. The placement of the NFFF memorial wreath now officially starts the weekend, and the nine months leading up to this day have involved concentrated, in-depth, and comprehensive planning for it. Fifteen minutes before the official start of the weekend activities and before the actual wreath placement ceremony is due to take place, I was antsy. Scores of thoughts were simultaneously running through my head regarding the events that had to be flawlessly managed in the next 30 minutes, let alone the next four days.

Jimmy, an incredibly special friend and close confidant, could see my angst. He turned to me briefly and said quietly, "Tim, you are the Commander. You have developed and communicated an excellent plan. You have created an incredible team. They will do anything for you. Let them honor you by their performance. Take it all in and enjoy the moment!"

That was quite an eye opener and a great reality check. I did just that, and it was another incredible moment that remains a highpoint of my leadership career. The wreath placement went perfectly, and it was another beautiful fall day as we once again looked down upon the Lincoln Memorial, Washington Monument, and U.S. Capitol building. Even Taps sounded a little more special that day.

Lastly, not everything at Arlington has to be solemn. There is always room for a little fire house humor. There was a young man from my fire department who felt compelled to do what was right, and he volunteered to serve in the army. While his Stryker squad was on patrol in Afghanistan, an IED (improvised explosive device) exploded next to them. Josh suffered multiple traumas, including shrapnel wounds, broken bones, and the loss of one of his legs. Once his medical condition was stabilized, he was transferred to the Bethesda Naval Hospital National Medical Center for numerous surgeries and rehabilitation. The hospital is located in Bethesda, Maryland, right outside Washington, DC. In 2011 Josh's recovery was progressing nicely. I invited him to attend the placement of the NFFF memorial wreath at the Tomb of the Unknowns in October. He was pleased with the invitation and enthusiastically accepted the offer. At this point in his recovery, Josh was still in a wheelchair with his "good" leg pinned in several places, and he wore a stainless-steel structure around his leg while the bones healed. He had not yet been fitted for a prosthetic device for his other leg.

I had recruited two of my close fire department honor guard colleagues to assist me with picking up Josh in our rented minivan. They were a little uncomfortable when they met Josh for the first time because (1) they didn't know him as well as I did, and (2) they weren't quite sure what to say. As they were assisting Josh into the backseat of the minivan, my colleague Hal said, "Can I give you a hand?" Josh's immediate response was "No, but I sure as hell could use a leg!" Four firemen were instantly bonded.

I should interject here that firemen are sometimes known for their gallows humor. We all had a good laugh, we slapped each other's backs, and relaxed. Josh commented that, like the Black Knight in *Monty Python and the Holy Grail*, "It's just a flesh wound." Josh was now one of us and we would do whatever it took to assist him with anything he would ever need—forever. Firemen are funny that way.

If you were to question where our country is going or how the next generation is going to manage, take a few minutes and have a chat with the Josh's of the world. Here is a young man who lost his leg serving our country and still wants to serve. While he assumes that the army will not grant his wish, he simply wants to be reissued his weapon and to be redeployed to Afghanistan to take care of some "unfinished" business. Having qualified for the U.S. Army marksmanship team, his next desire is to become a U.S. Army sniper. He acknowledges and appreciates the rigors of the sniper course but hopes that the army will give him an opportunity to qualify. If that doesn't work out, becoming an army drill sergeant is next on the list.

A proud American, a proud soldier, and a proud firefighter.

CHAPTER SIXTEEN

My Plan

"Let our advance worrying become advance thinking and planning."

—WINSTON CHURCHILL

I will be the first to admit that I have dealt with death more than most folk. Whether it was the passing of a family member, loved one, or the deaths of countless people I never knew during my fire service career, I closely handled each occasion with compassion. When thinking about death and funerals, no one sums it up better than Charles Dickens in *The Tale of Two Cities*:

> *"It was the best of times, it was the worst of times, it was the age of wisdom, it was the age of foolishness, it was the epoch of belief, it was the epoch of incredulity, it was the season of Light, it was the season of Darkness, it was the spring of hope, it was the winter of despair, we had everything before us, we had nothing before us, we were all going direct to heaven, we were all going direct the other way."*

I am the sole survivor of a family of five. My mother, father, sister, and brother have all died from disease. I am a firefighter. I have been to countless fatal motor vehicle accidents and too many fatal fires. I am a member of a special team that responds to major disasters around the country including school shootings, airliner crashes, and the attack on America on September 11, 2001. My most rewarding calling is bestowing high honors on my fallen fire service brothers and sisters and reaching out to support the needs of the surviving families.

In dealing with each of those situations there are always two inevitable questions that are asked. One of the questions I cannot answer, and the other question I can.

THE FIRST QUESTION IS WHY?

This is a question that is impossible to answer.

Why should disease ravage one body and not another? How can a specially trained, well-equipped, highly experienced firefighter not fully respect the hazardous environment he or she has entered into a hundred times before? What is a student's rationale for systematically shooting his peers? Why would a well-built, technologically advanced 747 aircraft fall from the sky? And why should nearly 3,000 innocent people, simply going to work on a beautiful September day, never have the benefit of ever seeing their loved ones again? I do not know, and I have long since stopped trying to rationalize irrational acts.

THE SECOND QUESTION IS: "NOW WHAT DO I DO?"

This question I can answer and *The Ultimate Family Gift* is the key.

This question is almost always asked by surviving family members when someone has died. I have heard it countless times. They are grieving, they are distraught, and they desperately want to regain some control over their lives. They urgently need a road map for what to do in the next 72 hours, the next 72 days, and the next 72 weeks.

Providing this guidance and the answers to this question is the mission of *The Ultimate Family Gift*. It is specifically designed with that goal in mind.

All that said, the development of this book did not come easily.

✓ HOT TIP

The most important concept to understand is that you can NEVER predict when you will die. Note: Your birth certificate does not come with an expiration date!

MY "GAS GAUGE OF LIFE"

As I compile the elements for this book, I am 65 years young. I have shared with you my family medical history. In spite of all the modern medicines and cutting-edge technologies, you should never overlook your own family medical history as you examine your personal health!

My dad died of prostate cancer at the age of 67. Does that have my attention since he was only a few years older than I am now? You better believe it! Semiannual physicals with digital rectal exams and PSA tests are now standard for me. And let's not forget the fun and joy of a colonoscopy. These physicals are never an enjoyable day, but a good defense is a strong offense. Do I expect to live beyond age 67? Absolutely! (But I am always looking over my shoulder.)

✓ HOT TIP ──────────────

Never overlook your family medical history when planning what the future may hold, and remember that some maladies skip a generation.

Celebrating our 40th wedding anniverary

Let's say I live to be 85 years old. That's a pretty good run. But any way you look at it, my "gas gauge of life" is down close to a quarter of a tank. Do I dwell on this reality at length? No, but those who know me well will acknowledge that one of my favorite sayings is, "Every day is a good day!" and I truly believe it.

"Aging is God's way of telling you that you don't have any time to waste."

—JAMIE LEE CURTIS

MY BUCKET LIST

If you have not yet seen the movie *The Bucket List,* I strongly encourage you to rent it sometime soon. The storyline revolves around two men, played by Jack Nicholson and Morgan Freeman, who are both terminally ill and reluctantly have to share a hospital room. They compile a list of all the things they would both like to accomplish before they "kick the bucket," hence the term bucket list. The movie tracks their humorous and stressful "vacation" around the world, fulfilling the wishes on their bucket lists.

Since I am down to a quarter of a tank on my "gas gauge of life," I too have created my own bucket list. I have always been a goals-oriented guy, and this endeavor is no different for me.

My bucket list:

- to walk my beautiful daughter down the aisle on the day she gets married;
- to make love with my beautiful bride on a beach in Tahiti as the sun slowly sets in the West;
- to snorkel on the Great Barrier Reef in Australia;
- to see the Northern Lights;
- to go on an around-the-world cruise;
- to shake hands with the president of the United States to thank him/her for being the leader of the greatest nation on the planet.

Create your own bucket list; it's an intriguing project! For a list of interesting suggestions visit www.timpelton.com/bucketlist.

MY PLAN

Well, as you may have surmised by now, my plan is pretty well established. Here it is:

First, my family has been a property owner at a local cemetery for over 20 years, waiting for the "big" day. Next, I want to be cremated. Now that might seem a little strange for a firefighter who has over 25 years of fire service experience. It is ironic to think that fire will finally "beat" me after all these years. Actually, that choice is based more on a personal business decision and looking at the return on investment. Why should my family invest in a $4,000 box that is only going to be used for 48 hours? I want to take that money and fund my very own "memorial roast."

Just what is a memorial roast, you may be asking yourself?

My memorial roast will be a large gathering of all my friends and family to share stories about me and to celebrate the past. It will entail copious quantities of food, alcohol, and fun. My primary objective is that there won't be a dry eye in the house, not from sorrow but from laughter. A number of speakers have already been identified to address this group with several, "Let me tell you about the time when Tim…" stories. I also have no doubt that many stories will be volunteered as well. At the end of the night, I'm hopeful there will be consensus that Tim was a "hellava guy" and a great wing man.

The funeral, however, will take on a little more structure. There will be a respectful service in a local church complete with honor guards, color teams, and all the accoutrements involved in a firefighter's funeral. Close family friends will do some readings, recite some letters, and wish me well. At the cemetery there will be bagpipers, a rifle team volley, Taps, and a flag-folding ceremony, all of which will be performed with high precision and stalwart military bearing by my colleagues on the Connecticut Statewide Honor Guard and at the National Honor Guard Academy.

And most importantly, I designed it all before Andy and I took the big off ramp!

CHAPTER SEVENTEEN

Call to Action

"Failing to plan is planning to fail."

—ALAN LAKEIN

Well there you have it. Let's begin to wrap up my goal of motivating you to think about your future. First of all, congratulations! Congratulations for having the courage to continue to read about a topic that is shunned, invokes fear, and is pursued with trepidation.

The primary purpose of *The Ultimate Family Gift* is to provide you with a firm but friendly reality check. Ben Franklin was right. "The only things certain in life are death and taxes."

✓ HOT TIP

The most important observation that I hope you take away from this book is that end-of-life planning is not about taking care of you but, more important, taking care of the survivors you will leave behind.

This is your official call to action.

1. Begin the challenging discussion with your family about what should happen when you or a loved one passes away.

2. Find the time to compile, assemble, and organize all the important documentation you may now keep in many different locations.

3. You're the head coach. Assemble your team and complete a written game plan.

4. Do it. Do it now. Do it today.

I am hopeful you found this book to be a great tool to get you to think about important personal information in an organized fashion that is easily accessible by your family. More important, your family will be both relieved and grateful that you took the time to outline your final wishes. Along the way I fully anticipate you may become uncomfortable with some of the subjects. It's okay. I understand. I have been there. However, I encourage you to stay the course and continue. The rewards at the end will be more than worth it. Remember, it's not about you. It is about all the ones you will leave behind. I am hopeful at this point that I have provided you with a call to action and convinced you that end-of-life planning is very important. I am passionate about your success. As most folks understand it, an exit interview takes place when employees move from one employer to another. It provides employees an opportunity to discuss with their employer what they liked about their job, as well as to comment on things that could make the job better. I want you to start to think in terms of how you want your ultimate exit interview to work.

IN CONCLUSION

I have shared my story with you to underscore that *The Ultimate Family Gift* is based upon a great deal of experience. For every fire department dispatch and every funeral event in which I have participated, I have always asked myself the question: "What went well, and what could we have done better?" Let me become your advisor as you begin to contemplate where to go from here. Let me help you remove the fog of denial surrounding dying and provide you a solution as you focus on your ultimate family gift. Dying is definite, why not have a plan.

My goal is to get you to start thinking that dying is as natural as being born. This book reflects all of those findings and more.

I am hopeful that sharing some of my experiences has challenged you to reflect and ask the questions:

1. What would I like to have happen for the rest of my life?
2. What do I want to have happen when I pass away?

Now it is your turn. Relax, and get started.

This book is my homework assignment to you. Go find your gift.

Have the bravery to begin discussing the tough questions. When you do, both you and your family will be fully prepared for your ultimate exit interview.

So much for me. Now it's your turn.

Okay, it's time to get to work.

Do not procrastinate!

Be well and remember that every day is a good day.

Need Some Additional Help?

"The way a team plays as a whole determines its success. You may have the greatest bunch of individual stars in the world, but if they don't play together, the club won't be worth a dime."

—Babe Ruth

As an owner of *The Ultimate Family Gift,* you now have exclusive access to a number of resources to help you get started. I have compiled a number of resources to assist you with planning for the rest of your life. All are available on my website **www.timpelton. com**.

Tim can also be followed on Linkedin, Twitter and Facebook.
Here is a sample of the offerings available:

- *Nine Ways to Start the Hardest Conversation Ever* is a 21-page report to assist you in broaching the challenging subject of what should happen when either (1) the inevitable is going to happen, or (2) someone is going into harm's way. It is a must read.
- *The 11 Things You Absolutely Positively Must Do before You Die* comprises 24 pages of insightful reading, organized in a descending order of priority—from #11 to #1. Also available at no cost on my website.

- *Terminal Programming* is a small report filled with important facts and punch list items every family should know about.

- *Time with Tim:* If you are not quite sure how to get started or have run into a delicate situation that requires a little coaching, I am available to serve as an objective advisor, and I will reassure you that you are doing the right thing. Arrangements can be made on my website at www.timpelton.com.

- Online videos are also available for all the planning elements described in this book, everything from strategic planning to having your ashes be part of a Fourth of July fireworks display. The videos are available at www.timpelton.com.

- Audio CDs are available. They feature interviews with attorneys, estate planners, insurance professionals, and funeral directors, all reinforcing why planning is so important. These audio files are also available at no charge on the website www.timpelton.com.

- Plus a whole lot more.

Don't forget to make your bucket list.

Come check out www.timpelton.com, I'm here to help you.

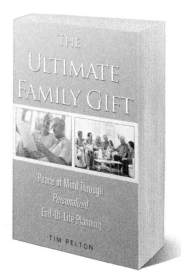

How can you use this book?

MOTIVATE

EDUCATE

THANK

INSPIRE

PROMOTE

CONNECT

Why have a custom version of *The Ultimate Family Gift?*

- Build personal bonds with customers, prospects, employees, donors, and key constituencies
- Develop a long-lasting reminder of your event, milestone, or celebration
- Provide a keepsake that inspires change in behavior and change in lives
- Deliver the ultimate "thank you" gift that remains on coffee tables and bookshelves
- Generate the "wow" factor

Books are thoughtful gifts that provide a genuine sentiment that other promotional items cannot express. They promote employee discussions and interaction, reinforce an event's meaning or location, and they make a lasting impression. Use your book to say "Thank You" and show people that you care.

The Ultimate Family Gift is available in bulk quantities and in customized versions at special discounts for corporate, institutional, and educational purposes. To learn more please contact our Special Sales team at:

1.866.775.1696 • sales@advantageww.com • www.AdvantageSpecialSales.com